LEANING WITH INTENT TO FALL

A MEMOIR

Ethan Clark

Garrett County Press first edition 2007
All rights reserved. No part of this book may be used or reproduced in any manner whatsoever without written permission from the publisher except in the case of brief quotations and embodied in critical articles and reviews.

For more information please address: www.gcpress.com
Garrett County Press books are printed on acid-free, recycled paper.
Printed in the U.S.A.
Special thanks to: Colleen McHugh, Jamie Schweser, Thomas Hancock and Dade Darby.

Interior illustrations by Ethan Clark.
Cover design by Claire Iltis
Cover photograph by Rebecca Nolan

Library of Congress Cataloging-in-Publication Data
Clark, Ethan.
Leaning with intent to fall : a memoir / by Ethan Clark. -- 1st ed.
p. cm.
ISBN 978-1-891053-04-7 (alk. paper)
1. Clark, Ethan. 2. Mississippi--Biography. 3. Asheville (N.C.)--Biography. I. Title.
CT275.C62165A3 2007
976.2'063092--dc22
[B]
2007017543

****

Publisher's Note: Names and identifying characteristics of individuals portrayed in Leaning with Intent to Fall have been changed.

****

Thanks to...Uh, all the usual suspects I guess...G.K., Jamie and Abram for riding me to make this thing for the last however many years, Tammy (duh), Happy, Casey, Dave and Janet, Shelley, everyone who is in these stories (thanks in advance for not getting mad about what I wrote), Krewe of Eris, Krewe Du Poux, and, uh ... Dead Moon, Gang of Four, Irma Thomas, Eddie Bo and Lee Dorsey for always being there. And New Orleans, despite our differences. OK. That's all (well, probably not, but all I can think of right now). OK.Word.

This book is dedicated to everyone who's ever dropped everything to go to New Orleans, everyone who's eaten out of dumpsters and everyone who's ever been arrested for assaulting a cheeseburger or leaning with intent to fall.

CONTENTS

Introduction	1
Fireworks	3
Kansas	27
Wild Dogs	41
Up Lee's Ass	51
Scenes from a Shattered Memory	81
Newness	123
Asheville – My Enabler, My Home	129
Sparks	137
Crack	143
Money	155
Suitcases	161
Hill People	167
High Life	176

INTRODUCTION

I've always been convinced that there are two types of writing in this world: There's the first type, the type that is carried simply by the action of the story. Books written like this keep you quickly flipping the pages with your gnawed-down fingernails, too busy wondering what will happen to the daring hero to notice whether or not the writer demonstrates strong use of alliteration. Then there's the second type of writing, which is carried by the writing itself. Books written this way could be about the most humdrum of topics – the trials and tribulations of a depressed phlebotomist, or "the love that almost was" down at the DMV – but they contain *something*, some kernel of human truth, that readers can personally relate to. This is the kind of book that gets read and re-read – and remembered – instead of ending up squished between the toilet and the wall in a pile so moldy you can no longer make out the plasma rifle that the space nymph is clutching on the cover. Eudora Welty had a quote about this writing phenomenon that really hit the nail on the head, though I can't remember what it was (despite the fact that it was framed on the wall of the bathroom at my parents' house, and I stared at it everytime I sat on the toilet throughout my adolescence).

I've tried to write stories this second way. The stories in here are about getting chased by wild dogs, about breaking into state monuments, about getting stuck hitch-hiking in Kansas and about stealing the wiring out of abandoned houses. Hopefully, though, these stories convey something more than that, convey some vague glimmer of truth that will lodge in the minds of anyone reading, not just those who have stolen the wiring out of abandoned houses or gotten stuck hitch-hiking in Kansas (and I'm not just saying this because people like that don't tend to buy many books). I know that I haven't completely succeeded, but if you read this book and think to yourself from time to time, "Oh yeah, I know what he's talking about! It *totally sucks* when that happens!" then I've accomplished my goal.

Oh, and everything in here that's illegal? That stuff is all made up.

—Ethan Clark

FIREWORKS

"WHATEVER HAPPENS after this," Taylor said, "let me point out that we are standing in Marshfield, Wisconsin, beneath a fireworks tent. And that, my friend, is a pretty amazing accomplishment." I agreed. While I realize there is nothing inherently amazing about standing beneath a fireworks tent in Marshfield, Wisconsin, the fact that we had made it there was mind-blowing.

It had been about two months since Taylor and I had been sitting in a pub in Ireland and had made shaky plans to work, as Taylor had done the year prior, selling fireworks during the Fourth of July season. Since Ireland, we'd traveled together to Amsterdam, and then returned home separately. Instead of going straight back to New Orleans, Taylor went to his hometown of Columbia, Missouri, and I went to New Orleans. Taylor had a number of unpromising conversations with a Wisconsin fireworks company, and it didn't look like our plan would materialize until the last minute. As soon as Taylor informed me that, yes, we had the job, I promptly broke my ankle while attempting to mount a six-foot unicycle.

"Well this is going to be fun," Taylor remarked as I hobbled off of a Greyhound bus in Columbia, Missouri.

"Shut up," I said, handing him my backpack and leaning on his shoulder for support. "I just rode the goddamned Greyhound for twenty-four hours. I always swear I'll never take it again, but then I do. I was in excruciating pain the whole time, with a drunk guy's head on my shoulder. You should be happy I'm here."

"Oh, yeah. Sorry. It's great to see you," said Taylor.

We were both broke, not to mention car-less, with only a couple of days left before we started the Wisconsin job. Had I been on my own, I would have thought that these were problems. Since Taylor had sold fireworks before, and since we were on his home-turf, I left the logistical aspects of our mission up to him. Taylor relied on his usual strategy: "Something will work out," he told me, and then we went to the bar. Between drinks, Taylor asked everyone he knew for advice on how we should make the eight-hour trip.

"You could sell kettle-corn by the highway," offered one acquaintance.

We're doomed, I thought.

Then Taylor asked his friend Jim if he felt like driving to Wisconsin. "I do," said Jim (…our heads perked up…) "but I have to work" (…and sank back down). The next morning, at Taylor's brother's house, the phone rang. Taylor rolled out of his nest on the couch and answered it. When he came back into the living room he said, "That was Jim. He says he took off work and asked if we could be ready in an hour." An hour later we were on the road, and eight hours after that, Jim was depositing us in the tiny town of Marshfield, Wisconsin, just so that he could turn around and drive back home. Thanks Jim!

We arrived the night before the tent was scheduled to open. On the way up, we'd swung by the warehouse of our employer, Christophe's Fireworks, a.k.a. "The Midwest's Largest Fireworks Company." There, at their warehouse, some be-mulleted Rowdy Roddy Piper look-a-like had given us our uniforms and the keys to a trailer full of fireworks. Thousands and thousands of dollars' worth of fireworks, without even asking our names. Taylor had told me about how, the year prior, he had to collect the money from tents in the towns surrounding his own tent. A woman responsible for a tent one town over had been completely shit-faced when he arrived at her motel, and her bag of money was thousands of dollars off. They'd tried to fix it (while the woman danced around in a Cat-in-the-Hat hat that she called her "fireworks hat") and had eventually given up. When they turned in the envelope, the company didn't notice the discrepancy.

If they're that irresponsible, I thought, surely they wouldn't miss one tent's worth of cash – or at least enough to get my ankle looked at.

Back in the car, I immediately began flipping through my address book looking for a potential candidate to come up to Marshfield and help us "rob" the fireworks tent. I had come up with three ne'erdowells in Milwaukee who probably had nothing better to do, but when I told Taylor my plan, he was quick to squelch my scheme.

"You do *not* want to fuck with these people," Taylor told me. "Our supervisor last year told me he always kept a gun under the seat of his Ryder truck, 'just in case.' If we rip them off, they won't call the cops. They'll handle it themselves. We'll be sitting in a bar in Madison or somewhere drinking Hamm's and a Ryder truck will come screeching out of nowhere, full of pissed-off dudes with shotguns and wraparound sunglasses. They will *hunt us down*."

How keen could these guys' detective skills be, I thought, when they didn't have enough sense to even ID us before putting us in charge of two tons of fireworks? *Their* fireworks?

Or maybe, I thought, that's their whole scheme. I mean, why else would they have hired two smelly scumbags like us to travel all the way to Wisconsin to sell their fireworks, anyway? Surely there's an eager workforce of local high school students up there, right? Maybe they just hired us so they could dangle the carrot of an easy scam in front of us and, when we inevitably took the bait and robbed them, they would get to wile away the off-season by tracking us down, kind of like that Ice-T movie, *Surviving the Game*.

Or maybe, you know, they're just disorganized.

Either way, I set aside my organizer and my dubious scheming. We rolled into tiny Marshfield at dusk. After checking out our tent, we checked into a motel up the street. The room, as well as all of our food over the course of the stay, was paid for by the company. This seemed unnecessarily generous, and confused me. I voiced my curiosity to Taylor.

"There's something I don't get," I said.

"What's that?" asked Taylor, flopping down on the bed by the window.

"Well…these guys are paying a lot to put us up in this motel and feed us. But why? I mean, this is a small town in the middle of the summer. There must be a whole army of bored high school kids just waiting to be tapped into. I mean, that's how all the corn in Iowa gets de-tassled: underage labor. They're paying us under the table anyhoo, we might as well be fifteen-year-olds that they don't have to get a motel room for."

"Don't waste your time looking for logic in the actions of the redneck mafia," he told me. "Just do whatever they tell us. Make sure the sparklers are priced right. Don't let anything catch on fire. We just have to make it until the Fourth, get our money and get out of Wisconsin."

So, I forgot about it (or at least stopped bugging Taylor about it) and we spent the rest of the evening celebrating our arrival by taking advantage of our complementary room and our complementary amenities. The festivities included a lovely warm bean dip (that we heated in the little Mr. Coffee in our room), sloppy, safety-pin-and-India-ink tattoos, a fifth of Jameson and a "Schlitz vs. Blatz" blind taste test.

The alarm clock/radio went off at eight the next morning and we were not, to say the least, in prime fireworks-selling form. Actually, eight o'clock came and went, but neither of us stirred. I do remember thinking, briefly, that it was odd I was being treated to my favorite classic-rock hits at eight in the morning, but it didn't take me long to stop worrying about it and go back to sleep. I woke again to Taylor's "Oh shit!" We had half an hour to get the tent's entire contents set up and to be open for business.

Four hours later, we had the tent set up and open. The memory of it is all a blur of cardboard boxes and packing material. Once Taylor declared that we were done, I was still trying to surface from a boozy haze. I looked out at the thousands of fireworks that we had just dragged from the trailer, unpacked, and stacked in picturesque pyramids. Rubbing my ankle, I wondered how I was going to get through two weeks of this; I marveled that we'd gotten it done once. I also marveled at the fact that we'd been in Marshfield for eighteen hours, and the company had no idea what we were doing in (or to) their tent. Hell, they didn't even know our names. The guy who'd hired us, Brian, had had such a hard time remembering Taylor's name that he'd requested Taylor just refer to himself over the phone as "Guy from Missouri." Soon this would be replaced by an umbrella title for both of us, which Brian would blurt at the beginning of each conversation: "Marshfield!"

Taylor called Brian to let him know the tent was set up. As he yelled, "This is the guy from Missouri!" into the little phone, I bopped over to our nearest neighbor, Arby's (a.k.a. "the bathroom"). When I returned, Taylor was staring at the phone with a dazed look on his face.

"Man," he said, "I just had the weirdest conversation with our boss." Apparently they'd had a bad connection. When Taylor asked Brian to repeat something he'd gotten no response.

Taylor: "Uh…hello?"

Brian: "Yeah, uh, what?"

Taylor: "What did you say?"

Brian: "Uh…I don't know. I have no idea what I said. Look, you need to call me later…I'm really drunk at Paul's house right now."

Click.

Apparently, this wasn't unprecedented behavior for the officers of Ye Olde Fireworks Empire, either: Taylor had regaled me with horror stories about Bud, his supervisor from the year before. Bud would storm into the tent on a daily basis to yell things like, "These displays look like shit!" or "You gotta shave! Come on, get on top of this shit!" And while a few days' stubble was apparently bad for sales, it was kosher for Bud to stand in front of the browsing families in the tent, screaming things like, "I'm sick of that bitch up in Steven's Point! I swear to shit that if she doesn't get it together I'm gonna go up there and slap the cobwebs outta her pussy!" into his phone.

Our new supervisor, Glen, showed up the afternoon of the first day. After hearing the Bud stories, Glen was a godsend. He was Brian's dad, a self-proclaimed "bored retiree" keeping busy by helping his son during the Fourth of July season. His job duties consisted mainly of roaming the Wisconsin countryside in a Ryder truck, making sure that each tent was in "tip-top shape." His shifts lasted about twenty hours, and it showed. Goddamn, could he talk. He talked like, well, like someone who spent twenty hours a day in the company of gunpowder-filled tubes. It was cool, though, because it became quickly evident that Glen would rather spend his brief visits with us, talking about fishing, than yelling about our facial hair. He certainly didn't seem like the type to go around slapping the cobwebs out of anyone's pussy. When he finally said goodbye and pulled out onto the highway in his Ryder truck, we decided that, due to Glen's fatherly demeanor, "Pappy" would make a good nickname for him. "I miss Pappy already," Taylor said, looking out at the highway.

That night we finished breaking the tent down and getting everything back into the trailer around ten-thirty, then loafed and limped back over to the Super Eight Motel. As Taylor counted the register, we drank a few cans of Schlitz (winner of the previous night's taste test) and ate an extremely mediocre pizza. This would become our nightly ritual for the next ten days, all we had to look forward to before another fourteen hour day beneath the tent, staring at one another in the Foods Festival parking lot.

The bright, windy days crept by, dragging us slowly toward *The Big Day*. Business increased steadily. More minivans and pickups careened into the parking lot and spewed forth families of fat, white Marshfudlians who all wanted one thing: The Good Stuff. See, it's like this: Due, no doubt, to some dark time in the town's history, the Great Roman Candle Massacre of '68 or something, Marshfield (along with much of the Badger state) had some pretty strict pyrotechnics laws. Our tent was what is known in industry jargon as a "Safe and Sane" tent, meaning we were not allowed to sell anything that left the ground or exploded. Trés lame, to be sure. One would think, though, that these four-by-four driving, gun-rack-toting pyromaniacs would be used to their town's oppressive explosive laws. Alas this was not the case. And instead of taking it up with their congressman, staging a coup or, at the very least, driving to another county for their Independence Day shopping, they just kept coming up to us and demanding the elusive Good Stuff.

Taylor, being the more seasoned fireworks-dealer between us, had predicted this phenomenon. Before leaving Missouri, a pyro's Promised Land of lenient laws, we'd picked up some of The Good Stuff. We'd blown fifty bucks or so on a bag of various M-80s, bottle rockets, tanks and the like, which we had hidden back at the motel. Since the fireworks company wasn't going to pay us until all was said and done, we hoped to hustle the contraband at just enough of a mark-up to provide us with beer money. When the first folks came sniffing around for The Good Stuff, Taylor pulled them aside and finagled a deal with them. They bought a few dozen of the M-80s, and the profit was quickly turned into more Schlitz.

A couple days later, though, our careers as firecracker smugglers, well, uh…blew up in our faces. I was chatting on the cell phone with Pappy, listening to more adventures of the bored retiree in mind-numbing detail. "I'm up by Wikitakata now," he was saying. "These kids wouldn't know the difference between a smoke bomb and a dadburn bologna sandwich…probably won't be making it down to Marshfield tonight. I'll probably stay outside of Tomahawk." When I finally faked a bad connection and wriggled out of the conversation, I found Taylor standing over the open register with his hands on his hips.

"What's wrong?" I asked.

"We, uh…we have a problem," he said.

Apparently the M-80 customers had returned, less than stoked about the quality of their purchase. It turned out that Missouri isn't really a Mecca of Good Stuff after all, more like a Limbo of Mediocre Stuff. I hardly saw how this was our problem, but Taylor had panicked and given them their cash back, which would have been no big deal, if either Taylor or I had any money. But we didn't. So Taylor'd reimbursed the unhappy shoppers from out of the drawer. Oof. The next couple days were spent pulling sketchy under-the-table deals, selling our inventory without actually ringing things up, and anything else we could do to make the register tape match the contents of the drawer.

Even with that taken care of, we still had to dump our bag of illegal fireworks. The fire marshal had come by several times, asking questions about our inventory, even getting our fingerprints to have on file. He let us know that they'd have people checking up on us regularly. All this pressure had made us increasingly paranoid about the bag of good stuff that we had hidden under the mattress in our hotel room. Then one day, we found our opportunity. This jovial, collegiate dude came in who said that he'd grown up in Marshfield but hadn't been back in a while. After perusing our wares for a minute, he noticed that something wasn't right.

"Hey, where's the bottle rockets and stuff?" he asked.

"We can't sell anything that leaves the ground or explodes," Taylor explained.

"Say what?" the guy asked. He gave us a cockeyed look, then turned his eyes upward, and shook a fist at the ceiling of the tent, bellowing, "GODDAMN YOU MARSHFIELD, WISCONSIN! YOU PISS ON ME AGAIN!"

I thought: I like the cut of this screaming man's jib. Twenty minutes later he was driving away with his bag of fireworks that were at least *louder* than anything we had in the tent, and Taylor and I had made enough to pay off the register and still get a twelve pack of Leinenkugels.

As soon as we exhausted our secret stash of unsafe and insane explosive, ground-leaving fireworks, the accusations from the customers that we were holding out on them got old really, really quick. The citizens of Marshfield are a stubborn, persistent lot with a hunger for explosions. They seemed to be under the impression that, if badgered enough, we would break down and say, "OK, follow me," and lead them to the underground vault where we kept the nuclear warheads. Maybe that's where the state got its nickname.

What really weirded me out about the whole "good stuff" phenomenon wasn't mankind's lust for explosion, it was this: While I'm not sure how to go about constructing, say, a fountain that showers blue crackling balls, I'm pretty sure that M-80s (along with Black Cats, bottle rockets and most of the other crap that the people of Marshfield were so hell-bent on illegally obtaining) are just little cardboard tubes with a bunch of gunpowder stuffed in 'em; you can buy all the ingredients at a hardware store. If you had such a deep need for crater-forming explosions, and you live in a town that you *know* doesn't allow them, why not just build your own damn fireworks? I was ready to shut the tent flap on the next pushy yahoo that came in demanding something other than the "kiddy shit" (as so many would-be customers described our inventory) on display.

Shit, I reasoned, if no one in this burg is industrious enough to do it themselves, maybe I should. I pictured my ideal black-market scenario. "Shit man," the customers would say. "This is all pussy shit! Where's the good stuff!" Then, shooting my eyes back and forth, I would quietly inform them that while we didn't have tanks or Roman Candles, I could still help them. "We do…" I'd say, reaching beneath the counter, "…have *this*." Then I would produce a large, hand-crafted pipe-bomb. To make it more appealing to consumers, it would have to have a gaudy label and a cute name, like "Parisian Subway," or "Olympic Park Surprise," perhaps. I'd show them how to detonate it with the wires sticking out the back and, if asked for a description, I'd tell them that "first, it shoots off a dazzling display of carpet tacks in every direction, followed by a blast of napalm. Basically, it rips your fucking face off." The allure of intense destructive capability, combined with the all-American need to celebrate how free we are (by breaking the law) would be too much for them to resist.

"Well, hell," these imaginary patriotic citizens would say, "give me two of 'em."

Lacking the supplies and start-up capital to actually see this fantasy plan through, instead, for a mere five bucks I offered to teach the citizens of Marshfield how to make their own pipe bombs. All I got were blank stares. So, all entrepreneurial fantasies quashed, I resigned myself to the redundant onslaught of questions:

"You got M-80s?"

"No."

"You got bottle rockets?"

"No."

"Do these leave the ground?"

"No."

"Does this explode?"

"No."

"You got any of those exploding Osama Bin Laden heads?"

"What? No!" (Though, unfortunately, they really do exist.)

What we had—*the only thing we had*—were fountains. I mean, yeah, there were a few smoke bombs, and some whipper-snappers, and those super-lame party popper things that don't work half the time. But mostly, fountains. Lots and lots of fountains. Fountains for every occasion, every possible pyrotechnic personality. There was the burly "Big Bad Ass

Fountain" fountain, the edgy "Hell Party" fountain, the surreal "Heavy Rhinoceros" fountain and the less-than-popular "Just Another Stinkin' Fountain" fountain. And though they all had their own unique, poorly-printed label, they were essentially all the same thing. This is what no one could grasp. When excited shoppers enter a fireworks tent, no matter their age, it's as though they suddenly lose the ability to either see or read. They stumble about, arms outstretched, knocking over displays and demanding to know, "What's this one do?"

"What does 'Mysterious Colors' do?" someone might ask, and I, who had never seen any of it in action, was supposed to have an answer.

"It, uh…changes colors," I would sputter, "*mysteriously*."

Taylor's advice on this was to take the constant probing as a challenge, a way to sharpen my skills of poetic sensory descriptions. I'm not big on poetry. Fortunately, I was reading a biography of Arthur Rimbaud at the time, and turned to the child-bard's mastery of sensual description for help. I walked around the tent, pairing descriptions with the book from labels that seemed to fit.

"Oh, *Creative Energy*," I'd say, practicing to myself, "It's a, uh, fountain that is, basically…*a rational derangement of all the senses*."

"Oh, you'll just love *Jumbo Cuckoo*," I pictured myself saying to some slack-jawed herd of shoppers, "*It whistles all day long through the boundless blue sky while a horrendous insanity pulverizes a million men into a steaming mass.*"

"Hey, Taylor," I called over the sparklers.

"Yes, Ethan?" he replied, looking up from one of the copies of *USA Today* that we picked up in the hotel each morning.

"What do you think Pappy would think if we started describing the fireworks with Rimbaud quotes? We could even put up little signs with the descriptions on them."

Taylor mulled it over for a minute before saying, "He'd probably tell you that a Baudelaire quote would be more suitable when describing 'Giant Lizard.'" Then went back to reading about Schwarzenegger's guberbatorial campaign.

Really, no matter who his preferred nineteenth-century French poet was, Pappy wasn't going to notice much of anything that went on under our tent. His system for keeping us in check and working hard was to keep referring to the "tent inspection" that could occur at any moment, any day. As you might imagine, this kept us neither in check nor working hard. Though we did try pretty hard to make the tent *look like* we were trying really hard.

Taylor, with characteristic fatalism, kept telling me, "It doesn't matter what we do: I guarantee that right when Brian shows up everything will go to shit. He'll walk in and everything in the tent will burst into flames or be full of rats or something." I hated this grim streak of Taylor's, but I hated it more when he turned out to be right.

The day of the dreaded inspection, Pappy called to warn us. "Stack 'em high, fellas!" he said, yelling over the sound of the wind as his Ryder truck rolled down some Wisconsin highway with the windows open. "Brian's making tracks toward Marshfield right now!"

Almost as soon as I'd hung up the phone, things started to go wrong. The wind picked up. The sky darkened and suddenly opened, dropping one motherfucker of a thunderstorm on our tent. We rushed to put up the storm sidings, huge heavy rolls of canvas that hung from the open sides of the tent. Hopping on my good leg, I pulled all of the boxes out from under the tables and away from the streams that were forming everywhere. It was as if Brian, Lord of the Fireworks Empire, was riding the wind out of the West straight toward Marshfield. Having still never met the man, I pictured some scruffy redneck dude wearing wraparound

Blue Blockers and thrashing the reigns of some great thunder dragon, the bursts of wind from its mighty wings uprooting trees while Brian yelled over his cell-phone, "Hey Paul, it's Brian! We getting drunk later or what?" with his golden mullet flowing behind him.

Obviously, I was let down when he showed up in a Ryder truck. Not only was he not riding any sort of mythical creature, he wasn't even the amphetamine-addled white-trash warlord that I had spent all that time building up in my head; he was just some dude that seemed like he'd rather be at home watching NASCAR than making sure all of our whipper-snappers were priced correctly. Luckily for him, he didn't have to. He'd brought along a secret weapon that we hadn't planned on: His daughter, who was anxious to prove herself as heiress to the Safe and Sane firework throne.

All Taylor and I could do was sit slack-jawed like the bumbling plebians we were as the eleven-year-old practically goose-stepped around the tent, telling us exactly what we were doing wrong. "This Secret Showers fell *over*," she snapped, waving the offensive fountain around before dropping it back on its side for us to fix. To the left of the register there were plastic bins full of the smaller fireworks like snakes and smoke bombs that were labeled with either orange or yellow tags to show their price. There, she stopped to take turns at each bin shoving her hands into the bottom and pulling out random smoke bombs and party poppers, hoping to find one that was, god forbid, priced with the wrong color tag. When Brian and Taylor stepped into the trailer to look at something, the girl turned to me.

"Once, when we were playing," she said, "I set my sister's clothes on fire with a sparkler." She spoke in a hushed voice with a tone so urgent that only a child could affect it convincingly. As she spoke, her mouth was expressionless and she kept her eyes honed on me, even after she was done talking. "She just went up!" she barked, snapping her fingers for emphasis. Just as she snapped, the heavy trailer door slammed shut behind me. I jumped. The girl smiled for the first time, then ran over to her dad.

Brian told us that everything looked good. "Ready pumpkin?" he asked his daughter.

"Yeah," she said, looking back at me one more time before climbing up into the Ryder truck.

Geez, I thought, as the big yellow truck pulled away. I would've preferred a thunder lizard.

After having our confidence whipped out from under us by a fifth-grader, we had little contact with the company. If we did, it was just from the fuzzy talks over the phone with Pappy. Rarely would he have news of any consequence for us, but he'd continue rambling on about his whereabouts and goings-on. Since our only other information from the outside world came from the pie-charts of *USA Today*, I came to look forward to these talks with Pappy and my days felt incomplete without them, like a bedtime story.

"What's Pappy doing?" I'd ask Taylor, if he'd been the one nearest the phone when it rang.

"Oh he's not gonna make it out today," Taylor'd explain. "Those damned kids out in Wassau weren't on top of their shit, so he's training replacements. He's gonna have to stay outside of Tomahawk tonight." As the days went on, it started to seem that Pappy was staying "outside of Tomahawk" more often than not — curious that a man as busy as old Paps would consistently wind up in the same town around bedtime. After all, Wisconsin's a big state. We theorized (having long since explored all other topics of conversation) that Pappy had a secret romance going on, a fling with some little firecracker outside of Tomahawk. Why else would he have taken the job? The company truck and the long nights put him in the perfect position for his little tryst. It made so much sense! He just better not let Brian's goose-stepping daughter find out about his flippant abuse of company resources; she'd probably sear off his lips with ground flowers.

Really, we only saw Pappy a few times. He'd swing by to collect the cash, which we counted and stuffed into manila envelopes. I'd taken over the financial duties for Team Marshfield after Taylor had nearly torn the hotel room apart over an accounting error. It was more than a little nerve-wracking. Each night, when the customers cleared out, we'd start closing. Taylor would use his two good ankles to start packing everything up (which, even when done with total recklessness, took over an hour) while I'd sit behind the register squinting at a calculator in the waning sunlight. And each night, one thought would stick in my brain that would distract me from the task at hand: I am sitting in a dark parking lot with six thousand dollars in my lap. And there is no culture, anywhere on planet Earth, that would consider that "smart." I kept looking over at Arby's, half-expecting some employee, some highschool aged kid fed-up from serving one-too-many strawberry shakes to one-too-many assholes, to come beat us down and wipe us out. It wouldn't have taken much; had we been threatened with, say, a bag of frozen curly fries, we would've handed the cash over whole-heartedly.

At the end of each night, when the money was counted and stuffed in the envelope, we were supposed to fill out the comments section printed on the outside of the envelope. I was never quite sure what was supposed to go in the comments section. At first I wrote normal stuff: "Weather was good. Business steady," or "Ran out of orange pricing tape." But soon that got boring and I started getting a little more creative. I figured that whoever was on the receiving end of the comments, after several hundred that said "Business is good" would probably appreciate the flourishes.

"Lots of customers today," read the first of the improved envelopes, "but it sure gets lonely out here on the far end of Marshfield. So very, very lonely." A second along the same vein read, "Why doesn't she love me anymore?" and a third, scrawled in a spasm of alienation halfway through our stint in the tent said, "WHO ARE YOU???"

The customers, in the throes of firework fever, hardly noticed that we were there, and offered little respite from our disconnectedness. There are only a few that I even remember: An old guy told us about the days of his youth when selling fireworks was done clandestinely, one day a year, out of the back of a truck. "And they were like friggin' hand grenades!" he said. He looked around at our stock. "Things now are just so much… tamer." Another time a couple walked into the tent, each with a lit cigarette hanging from their mouth. Taylor and I just stared, slack-jawed, as they proceeded to browse until I pulled myself together and yelled, "You can't smoke in here!" They looked at me, then down at their cigarettes before it registered with them. "Oh yeah," said one, "Huh, huh. I guess that's a bad idea, huh?" For the most part, though, the customers were less than memorable. To them, we were seen as little more than change-and-bag-dispensing automatons. To us, they were obstacles that stood in the way of our getting to sit down. The dialogue beneath the tent was an endless loop that I could hear even at night when I finally made it to the starched white sheets of my bed at the Super Eight.

"Everything with an orange tag is two for the price of one."

"Is this orange?"

"No, that's yellow."

"Where's the good stuff?" Etc., etc., etc.

Occasionally one or both of us would have these kind of breakdowns in front of customers and start spurting whatever popped into our heads. One day, some wise-cracking dad had come into the tent, making jokes to impress his kids. When I failed to respond to the guy's antics he said, "Boy, you sure look excited!"

"That," I calmly informed the gentleman, "is because I hate my life."

It didn't phase him, though. These vocal spasms never seemed to phase any of the customers; they sidestepped our despair the way that pedestrians sidestep panhandlers. I could have screamed, "Help me, I'm in hell!" and the customer would have said, "So…who do I make this check out to?" Once, though, a woman asked Taylor what one of the fountains did, and he answered honestly, "I have no idea what it does. Actually I don't know what any of them does. I've never seen them." And the woman angrily accused us of being on drugs and stormed out.

And so it went, all day, every day, until the Big Day finally arrived. That morning there was a little extra bounce in my limp, and as we unpacked the trailer in the morning, the sun looked more glorious than any fireworks display could. We were getting out of there! The Fourth was hectic and tiring, but not really any different from all the other days in the parking lot. Plus we knew, with every box we lugged, every time we explained that nothing in the tent left the ground or exploded, that it got us closer to being done. Done with the price tags, done with the rednecks in their Ryder trucks, done with the Festival Foods, the Super Eight and the goddamned fireworks tent. When the sun began to set, and as all the fireworks we'd distributed began to go off in Marshfield (plus some that sounded suspiciously as though they might be leaving the ground *and* exploding), I counted down the money. It was a lot of money, so much that it barely fit in the envelope. I got it in, though, and as Taylor loaded what little merchandise was left back into the trailer, I wrote my final installation of the comments section. It said, simply, "I need a drink."

We had to get up early the next day to do inventory and whatnot, but soon we said, "To hell with it!" We were celebrating. That night we were going out on the town. We'd been looking forward to it all day.

"We're going to to-own. We're going to town!" I sang as I priced the last of the Space Lamps.

"I wish I had a new hat to wear!" Taylor said, followed by a little jump and click of the heels.

Back at the motel we showered and shaved. We stuck what little beer money we had left over from our various schemes and scams in our wallets and headed down to the lobby. We called a cab from Marshfield's only cab company, but it never showed up. We weren't discouraged, though, and decided to hoof it. My ankle still hurt like all hell, but even if I'd been paralyzed from the waist down I probably would've clawed my way down the sidewalk with my hands just to get away from that same strip of highway and parking lots we'd been staring at all along. As we walked, the big Marshfield fireworks display was ending somewhere behind us, a dull glow rising above the trees. Soon after, the highway became flooded with trucks, minivans and SUVs as everyone in the county poured out of the fairgrounds and headed home.

The first drinking establishment we came to was empty except for the woman running the place who was full of liquor and, for reasons unknown, visible contempt for us. The second place we went was tended by a jovial guy who greeted us by yelling, "The fireworks dealers! I saw you guys in the paper!" We were celebrities! That place was ok, but we couldn't stay. We had places to go.

Before we'd started working at the tent, when our friend Jim had driven us into town, we'd seen one place that had piqued our interest. It was pretty far away, but we made the walk, with Taylor occasionally helping me along. We passed most of the main business-y stuff on the strip: furniture stores, City Hall, the police station. We passed railroad tracks and drunken revelers. We passed abandoned buildings and car dealerships. We passed other fireworks tents in various stages of dismantlement. Finally, we reached our destination, the oh-so-mysteriously named bar on the edge of town, "NUTZDEEP II."

The place was a huge, antiquated brick building. A neon "Old Style" sign buzzed in a steel-mesh-covered window. We stood for one final moment of wonder about the place before going inside. I imagined NUTZDEEP II to be the heart and soul of the Marshfield nightlife, the type of place where epic romances blossomed and collapsed, where working-class poets scribbled their songs of hope and triumph in corner booths, where boys named Sue had violent reunions with their estranged fathers. Yes, I expected nothing but greatness from NUTZDEEP II. My hand shook slightly as I reached for the heavy wooden door with the peeling paint. My heart pounded in my ankle, and we went inside.

Man.

What a letdown.

NUTZDEEP II *totally* sucked.

Everyone inside the place stopped to stare at us as we crossed the threshold into the gaudy, fluorescent-lit sports bar. Not only was it the kind of place where everyone stops what they're doing to gawk at strangers, I think that they stop what they are doing to gawk every time that the door opens, just on the outside chance that it *is* a stranger. We walked through the room to the huge wraparound bar, and they *kept staring*. Sure, Taylor and I probably would've done well by a roll of quarters and a trip to the Laundromat, but we really weren't too freakish. By the looks on their slack-jawed faces, though, you would've thought that we'd climbed out of the swamps and were demanding all of Marshfield's virgins while speaking through our gills.

"Maybe they saw us in the paper," I whispered as we walked through the gauntlet of gawking faces.

"Uh, can I get two Pabsts?" Taylor asked the bartender.

Eventually the place resumed its business. Conversation and games of pool resumed. Drinking carried on. It still sucked, though. We at least thought we'd get a good story about the place's name, but when Taylor asked about it, he just got blank stares. The woman behind the bar, a middle-aged lady with big red hair and dangly hoop earrings, stopped in the middle of wiping down the bar. She cocked her head and still holding a grimy towel, put both hands on her hips.

"Huh," she said. "Know what? I never really thought about it before!"

She turned toward the back of the bar and called to someone out of sight, presumably her barback, or the cook, perhaps. "Hey, Linda!" she yelled, "Linda!" Linda came out of the back room, a plump woman in her late twenties in a dumpy sweatshirt.

"Yeah? What?" she asked.

"You know what NUTZDEEP II means?"

She did not.

"Well," I asked, "Is there a NUTZDEEP I?"

The two of them shrugged. "I really don't know," said the first woman, who went back to wiping the bar.

Goddamn you, Marshfield, Wisconsin, I thought. You piss on me again. Disappointed, we said goodbye to NUTZDEEP II and headed back toward our end of Marshfield, Pabsts still in hand.

Limping along, I thought about our adventures. Before selling fireworks, when Taylor and I were in Europe together, we had hitch-hiked across England and eventually stayed with friends in a squat in Amsterdam. There, we spent our days riding around on bikes we'd fixed up, eating organic produce picked from the trash. That's what everyone we met did, too. Everywhere we went, people were reusing: reusing bike parts, reusing abandoned buildings. There were more bikes than cars, and people traveled on separate roads for bikes, hauling their laundry, their kids, even moving all of their possessions to their new homes. There were gardens everywhere. That's the culture, and surely it is one of the most efficient countries on Earth. Now, I thought, we're here. Marshfield, Wisconsin. USA concentrate.

The SUVs were still clearing out, heading the thirty miles back home at nine miles-to-the-gallon. The fireworks popped and cracked and showered and exploded all around us, burning for a brief second before turning to a pile of charred trash. I pictured the fat faces staring into them, glowing red, white and blue. They were the same faces that had spent ten days asking us, "What does this one do? What does this one do?" to which we had no answer. But there, half-drunk and stumbling down that sidewalk, I realized what it is that the fireworks do, what they all do. Sure, they "emit colored sparks and crackles," like it says clearly on the package, but it's more than that. That's not why the Fourth of July and New Year's Eve turn people into these roving mobs willing to empty their wallets for the things. It's because, for that brief moment that they are lit, for that small chunk of your paycheck, they let you forget. You can stare into the flames…and forget. Forget about your problems, and the problems of your country. Forget about the war that spews out of your car's gas tank. Forget about the glaciers. Forget about the forests. Forget about the lies we are fed each day, and be thankful. Be thankful for your God-given rights as an American: Your right to blow money on sweatshop-made fireworks, for example, or running shoes or CDs, or whatever. Be thankful for your right to put that gas in your car. Or your right to sit in some shitty bar with a weird name and drown it all out, for that matter. Your right to Wal-Mart, to Pepsi, to the million strip-malls in a million towns like Marshfield, to as much McDonald's, Pizza Hut and Taco Bell as you can stuff in your face. Your God-given right to buy, buy, buy. Be thankful for your God-given right to work hard and spend money on all of the colored sparks and crackles that America has to offer. All of the colored sparks and crackles that our poisoned hearts could ever desire.

KANSAS

THE CARS BLEW PAST ME, one after another, without even slowing down to read my sign. I'd been standing on the on-ramp for going-on seven hours beneath a cloudless sky. The July sun hung above me like a guilty conscious, and had lightened my hair and darkened my skin so that they were not only the same color as each other, but also as the brown Kansas plains behind me.

No wonder no one is stopping for me, I thought. They can't even see me anymore.

I hoped that vultures might start circling over me soon and provide a little shade. I thought about the manic pinball-bounce that I'd been doing around the middle chunk of the country. A pair of hippies had brought me to Kansas late the night before. They'd picked me up on an exit with no buildings in Colorado. Initially I'd been headed to Portland after working at the fireworks tent in Wisconsin. I'd gotten a ride out of Iowa with a lonely drunk guy who had just been heading to the movies but decided, instead, to drive me to Portland. In Nebraska, though, his courage (not to mention the Miller High Life he'd been swilling out of a sixty-four ounce Big Gulp cup) wore off, and he'd dropped me back on the highway. Discouraged and slightly freaked out by the guy for reasons I didn't entirely understand, I'd taken a ride to Boulder, Colorado, then U-turned to go see Taylor in his hometown of Columbia, Missouri, so that we could return to New Orleans together. It was dusk and, having given up on getting a ride, I'd settled into my new home by spreading my art supplies out around me on the asphalt and working on the comic strip I was drawing. I didn't stick my thumb out, and after a while even stopped looking up when the occasional car did pass. So when a red SUV with a couple of hippies inside blew past, I barely spotted them out of the corner of my eye. The words "fucking fake-assed hippies" just had enough time to run through my head when the SUV slammed on its brakes and lurched into reverse.

As they backed up toward me I thought: oh great, now these hippies have read my thoughts and are backing up to run me over. It seemed like a logical progression for the plot of my life, one more pain-in-the-ass thing to happen to me while hitch-hiking. But no, they just hadn't seen me, bent over my sketchbook like I was, until they'd passed. The red Wagoneer stopped right in front of where I sat and the driver, a guy in a fleece pullover with big dreadlocks and glasses, hopped out smiling.

"Whoah, man," I said, scooping handfuls of pens and pencils off of the road, "I've never seen anyone back up to pick up a hitch-hiker before!"

"Well, brother," said the guy as he helped me grab my bags, bell-hop style, "you ain't never met me!"

His traveling companion was a girl who looked like his twin sister, with big red dreadlocks tied back into a knot, the same as his. They drove fast, blasting Elton John the whole time, and took me to a farm that belonged to her father. He was a corn farmer, and as a hobby he had dynamited out the ground behind his house, and built a swamp in its place. Over the swamp was a weathered boardwalk that connected a bunch of little cottages that he'd fixed up and littered the property with. They'd put me up in one of these, which was decorated with quilts, sets of Reader's Digest Condensed Books, and a bottle of Jack Daniels, which I drank. The corn farmer had fed us corn, and we called it a night. In the morning he fed us corn again.

The hippie couple had said they would take me to the interstate, but our exodus from the corn-farm was postponed due to a debate that went like this:

> *Hippie Guy:*
> *I remember when I was a kid, always going to some place around here that was shaped like a big ice cream cone.*
>
> *Corn Farmer:*
> *Naw, not around here you didn't.*
>
> *Hippie Guy:*
> *Yeeeeah, I did. It was pink with a big old white ice-cream-top for a roof.*
>
> *Corn Farmer:*
> *Naw, I ain't ever seen that.*
>
> *Hippie Guy:*
> *Yeah, it's right around here somewhere, I swear.*
>
> *Corn Farmer:*
> *Naw...maybe over in Tanner it is, but not around here.*
>
> *HippieGuy:*
> *NO! I remember, it was pink ...*

… And so on and so on. Finally they admitted stalemate and we got back into the SUV to continue our trek eastward. They dropped me at the intersection of two state highways and pointed the way toward the interstate, *my interstate*, saying, "It's just down there. Someone will pick you up, no problem."

I cringed at this obvious curse.

The hippies hugged me and wished me luck. And then they were gone, leaving no trace except for a twenty they'd slipped in my pocket and the lyrics to "Tiny Dancer" in my head. Suddenly it was just me, the morning, and the big Kansas sky. This isn't so bad, I thought, sticking out my thumb. Just a guy, out here, on his own, seeing the world…Doing things my way…Yeah, wow, I'm really tough. This is so fucking cool.

An hour later, though, I was still walking, getting passed by one big rig after another. It wouldn't have been a big deal, but a few weeks before, I'd had an unfortunate unicycle accident, which had left me with a severely sprained or broken ankle that made walking difficult. It seemed as though I could see forever on the flat plain, but the interstate was nowhere to be found. Each mile caused my ankle to throb a little more, and the sun got bigger and bigger above me.

When hitch-hiking is good, it's great, and I'd had some pretty legendary rides: The guy who had no money or seemingly even any shoes, who was just driving aimlessly around the country and took me four hundred miles out of his way, letting me sleep in the cab of the truck at night. The couple in a RV who drove me from Colorado to California and let me have my own bed. There were rides that gave me food, beer, took me home to their families. There was the prison guard in upstate New York who lectured me the whole ride about how it was okay for me to live off of the excess now, but someday I would have to buckle down and fly right. Then he gave me twenty bucks and a carton of cigarettes. When you get those rides it really feels like you're getting over on the world, like you really don't need cars or money or jobs or any of it. More often, though, there are the bad times. There's the stuck-in-rain times, the hungry times, the one-too-many creepy dudes picking you up times. These are the times where those strangers' couches, those shared fast-food French fries, those acts of kindness that you'd experienced before seem so far away and it's as though, perhaps, your ride karma is all used up, and you never gave anything back, and maybe if you hadn't ordered the Biggie Fries that one time when that one lady bought you lunch, but no, you did. And now you're never going to get picked up again.

And, of course, once you start thinking like this, things just get worse, which it did in Kansas. It started to feel as though the big rigs were all speeding up as they passed, probably sniggering about the funny looking limping guy to each other over their CB radios. My ankle was killing me, I was waterless and the corn breakfast wasn't really sustaining me. Plus I was beginning to doubt the existence of the freeway. Something had to be done. I opened my backpack and pulled out some clothes, art supplies, and a book and scattered them across the shoulder of the road and in the grass, and then I lay down, face down, in the middle of it all.

And I just lay there.

For a long time.

No one stopped. I began to fear that someone might actually swerve over and hit me just to make *sure* that I wasn't getting back up.

I cannot believe, I thought, that I live in a world where people in their big rigs or their SUVs or their sports cars will just fly by, leaving someone lying on the damn highway!

I lay there for a while longer, getting angrier and angrier as traffic roared past.

And then I lost it. I jumped up, ignoring the shooting pain from my ankle, and to keep from exploding, took out my rage on the nearest available object, which was a speed limit sign. I was screaming and jerking the sign back and forth, trying to tear it out of the accursed Kansasian dirt, and good progress was being made—I almost had it out—when I heard something behind me. No way, I thought. Then I turned to discover that, yes indeed, it was a car — a car that had stopped to give me a ride. Me: the screaming, raving maniac with the road sign in his hands. I gathered my possessions off the ground, scooped them into my bag and ran over to the little sedan. The driver was a middle-aged guy in sunglasses, smoking a cigarette and looking like he was on his way to work.

"Whoah, hey, thanks man…I'm just going to the interstate," I said, hopping in.

"I'll take you there," he said, then added, "People around here don't pick up hitchhikers."

"Yeah…I noticed," I told him. "I was having a little bit of a freak-out back there."

He glanced over his shoulder until he could merge back into the traffic of the highway. "Yeah," he said, " I noticed."

He dropped me near the ramp to the interstate and wished me luck. As he took off, I checked out my new digs. There were three buildings at the exit: a gas station, a tourist-trap called "Prairie World" with a sign boasting "World's Largest Prairie Dog!" and a boarded-up building shaped like a big pink ice-cream cone. Pretty bleak. Limping down the on-ramp, I took my position. It's illegal to stand on the interstate proper, though people do it. Usually I just stand as close to it as I can, in a spot that could still arguably be considered on the ramp if a highway patrolman were to stop.

This I did.

I stuck my thumb out.

And there I stood.

And stood.

And stood.

There hits a point when you're hitchhiking, when you've been staring at the screaming traffic for so long that the glare from the windshields gets burned into your retinas. You see it when you close your eyes, along with the blurred faces of the motorists. Someone once said to me, "There's two types of people in this world: those who'll pick me up hitchhiking, and those who won't." And there are several types of *those* people who *won't* pick you up, and you get to know them well. There are those that give you the innocent, "I would if I could!" shrug. There's the Frantic Pointing, meant to indicate, "I'm only going to the next exit!" These are annoying, but at least well-meaning. On the other end of the spectrum are the Antagonistic Drivers, the ones who give you the finger, screaming "Get a car, faggot!" (because, apparently, carlessness equals homosexuality). Or the Teasers, the ones who pull over long enough for you to get within arm's reach of the passenger door before speeding off, spraying you with gravel and, sometimes, beer cans. Then there are the Ignorers, the ones who suddenly, upon spotting you, become extremely interested in the scenery on the opposite side of their car, or with their CD booklets. In some ways, these people make me angrier than the straight up assholes, because they are the ones too cowardly to look into the face of this fellow human that they know they are leaving stranded.

It turns out that Kansas is full of those people.

As they crossed under the overpass and saw me, so many of the passing drivers suddenly swiveled their heads to avoid eye contact that I was afraid of indirectly causing an accident.

Maybe I'm doing something wrong, I thought. Maybe I'm not hitchhiking *hard* enough.

I gritted my teeth, flexed my neck and forced my thumb-arm

out as far as it would go. This, of course, just made me look like some amphetamine-addled freak, and didn't prompt anyone to pull over and let me in their car. Next, I tried to communicate with the drivers through notes. In the notebook I was using as my journal, I wrote, "MISSOURI," and held it up. After an hour or so with no success, I wrote, "I KNOW YOU'RE GOING TO MISSOURI!" but that, too, got surprisingly little result. Over the course of two more hours I covered a small tree farm's worth of pages with my messages:

"SMELLY BUT FRIENDLY!"
"UNARMED!"
"KNOW GOOD JOKES!"
and eventually just:
"HELP!"

When someone finally stopped, it was a guy returning home from California after a business trip. Unfortunately, his home was only one on-ramp away.

"There's a big truck stop there," he told me. "You'll probably have more luck." On the way up to the next ramp, he made awkward small talk. "Did you go see the World's Largest Prairie Dog?" he asked.

"No, I didn't make it over to Prairie World," I said. "Have you seen it?"

"Nope, never have. It must be getting real old, though, it's been there as long as I can remember."

He dropped me off at the next exit and waved as he rolled away. The "truck stop" that he'd thought would treat me better was actually a weigh station, which was closed. Thinking I'd been better off before, I hitched back, this time with a middle-aged woman who thought I'd actually have better luck on the on-ramp *before* the one I'd been on all day. She too asked me about the prairie dog and she, too, had yet to actually see the thing herself. She dropped me off at a ramp that did have a sizeable truck stop on it, plus a couple of hotels. This was the main exit of Colby, Kansas, and it looked pretty promising.

I held up one of my many notes and waited. A few minutes later, there was a rustling in the bushes behind me. I braced myself for a giant prairie dog attack, and was a little disappointed when it turned out to just be some guy. He was a middle-aged guy with a Confederate flag doo-rag, a scraggly beard, and a pair of fluorescent orange Ray-Ban knock-offs. He was wearing a big pack and had a little boom-box hanging around his neck blasting classic rock.

"This guy is not doing what I think he's doing," I thought. "He is *not* hitch-hiking." But there was no way, really, that he could've been doing anything else. From head to toe, the guy screamed "I spend a lot of time on on-ramps." You don't see guys like this anywhere but on on-ramps, in fact. If a cop were going to go undercover as a hitch-hiker, he would dress like this guy. I watched dumb-struck as as he walked up to the edge of the on-ramp, about ten feet down from me, and, sure enough, stuck out his thumb.

This is not going to help me get out of here, I thought. I stood there for a minute, unsure of what, exactly, was proper etiquette in this situation. Finally, reasoning with him seemed the only option, and I walked down to where he stood.

"Hey man," I said. "Look, I've been here all day and —"

"HUH!?" he yelled, turning down the Creedence Clearwater song blaring from his little radio.

"I said, I've been standing here all day, and I'm having shitty luck. There's no way anyone's going to stop if we're both here."

He just stared at me through the orange sunglasses, in which I could see my own expectant face. I began to explain my position again, when someone did, actually, stop.

It was the law.

"How you boys doing?" said one of the two cops, a lean, blond guy with a white smile that seemed blinding against the brown backdrop of all that Kansas.

"Swell," I mumbled. My new pal said nothing.

"You boys got any ID?" asked the cop, while his partner stood behind him with his arms crossed.

"Yes," I said. "Have we done something wrong?"

"Oh no," said the smile, "It ain't that. I just want to know who you are in case you show up dead." He took both of our IDs and went to his car to run them. As he did, a battered red pickup pulled over to pick us up. The cop returned our IDs, and me and the doo-rag guy squeezed into the cab. Our drivers were a young kind of punk-looking couple, a guy and a girl. The girl, a tiny redhead with tattoos on her hands, was driving.

"We aren't really going anywhere," she said, but I couldn't hear her over doo-rag's blaring, crackling FM radio.

"What?" I hollered.

"We're not going anywhere!" she said louder. "We just wanted to piss off those cops because they're assholes! I'll take y'all a couple ramps up, though."

"Oh, that's cool," I said, getting used to the fact that none of the cars that had been passing me all day were actually *going* anywhere. The couple drove us back to the ramp with the closed weigh station. "Look," I said, "can you actually take me back one more?"

"Sure," said the girl driving. Doo-rag got out, taking his classic rock racket with him.

On the way back the three of us chatted. It turned out that we had acquaintances in common. The girl driving, though from Kansas, lived in Seattle and was just back taking care of her sick mom. The guy in the middle still lived there, and they'd gone to high school together. They told me stories about how fucked up Colby was, especially the cops, and gave me their phone number if I needed a place to stay. "You want me to drop you by Prairie World?" asked the girl.

"Yeah, that's fine."

"You been to that place?"

"No," I said, "but I've heard a lot about it. No one I've talked to has actually seen the big prairie dog, though."

She pulled the truck over on the on-ramp that I'd gotten to know so well earlier. "I've seen it," she said.

"What, really?"

"Yeah, it's fucked up. You pay seven dollars, right, and there are all these sad looking animals in cages, and then as you're leaving, the prairie dog is above the door."

"How big is it?"

"About this big," she said, holding her hands about two and a half feet apart. "And it's *stuffed*."

"What? Really? It isn't even alive?"

"Nope, it's stuffed and standing there with its arms up like this." She held her arms up, fingers spread like claws, making a threatening face.

"Whoah. That's so lame!" I said.

"Yup."

I hopped out, resuming my position. My spirits were up from my positive encounter with the punk couple, but the ball of fire that had baked me all day was about to set. I looked up at Prairie World, where that stuffed prairie dog had been for so long, fooling people. I knew nothing good was going to come to me in Colby, Kansas.

Maybe in the morning things will look up, I thought, and went to find somewhere to sleep. First, though, I had to run an errand. I walked away from the highway, past a few fast-food places, paint stores and a Wal-Mart. At a gas station, I went in to buy a beer, but, as I'd suspected, the beer was all 3.2 percent alcohol. For those not familiar with the phenomenon known as "3-2 beer," it isn't really *real beer*, but a foul, flat-tasting approximation that states with barbaric liquor laws try to pass off as beer. Dejectedly, I bought a tall can of the stuff.

In the parking lot, though, I had a new idea. I approached a woman about to get into her minivan. She had a beehive haircut coiled on her head like some fat snake, and was smoking a long, skinny menthol.

"Excuse me," I said as politely as I could. She stared at me. "Uh…is there a liquor store in this town?" I asked.

She took a long drag off the cigarette, looking me over from tattered sneaker to sun-baked face. "Yeah," she replied finally, "but you gotta have a *car* to get to it."

Oh, Jesus Christ! I thought. That's it! That's enough. I'm not tough. I'm not freewheelin'. I'm not anything. I never should have listened to those Woody Guthrie albums when I was a kid, and I just have to get out of Kansas! Away from this town of ice cream-shaped buildings, cops, giant prairie dogs and shitty beer! And I decided to subject myself to something I'd sworn off forever.

"Well then," I said to the woman, "Is there a Greyhound station?"

"Oh yeah," she said. "I can definitely tell you where that is." Which she did.

I counted what little money I had, then limped over, with my tail between my legs, to the bus station. I spent my life savings on a bus ticket, sat outside, waiting, drinking my 3-2 beer.

Six hours later, I left Kansas behind.

WORLD'S LARGEST!

WILD DOGS

THE MAIN THING that frightens people when I describe my neighborhood in New Orleans isn't the drug dealing, or shootings, or muggings, or even the influx of yuppies. It's usually when I mention the wild dogs that I get the slack-jawed stares.

"Wild dogs?" say Mississippians that I went to high school with when telling them about what I'm up to.

"Wild dogs?" say my middle-aged suburban relatives before quickly veering the conversation toward a more suitable subject.

"Wild dogs?" say friends from Iowa City, the small Midwestern college town where I spent several years, who actually think that having anything in your neighborhood other than frat boys and snow sounds pretty good.

But everyone is equally amazed and I find myself saying things like, "Well, yeah, sure, there are some wild dogs in our neighborhood that, sometimes, when we ride our bikes by where they hang out they, well, try to, uh…*catch us*. But you know, they're alright. It's a great neighborhood, really. You should come visit!"

So far the only takers have been the ones who didn't know about the wild dogs.

There used to be lots of wild dogs, roving packs of them that would knock over trash cans, and block traffic to come stand around my home, a giant Dodge Ram conversion van, barking at my own dog. This could sometimes put a damper on the coffee shop job I had. Try explaining to your boss that at five-thirty in the morning you were being held hostage by two chows and a terrier and *that's* why you couldn't get the shop open by six like you were supposed to. It doesn't go over so well. (Although my employer, Glenn, was a big fan of talking about how messed up my neighborhood, the Ninth Ward, was, and would often greet me in the morning with articles he'd cut out about various Ninth Ward atrocities.)

Lately, it seems that the roaming packs of delinquent canines have gone the way of the hundred-and-twenty-five dollar apartments, the resident families, and the neighborhood feel that was so prevalent even a couple of years ago when I moved here. This neighborhood is now "up and coming," with more and more white professionals every time you blink, more and more businesses, more and more cops, more and more arrests. There's a Ninth Ward website, for Christ's sake.

Perhaps the major dog-posses have just been pushed out, over the Industrial Canal, or above St. Claude Avenue. There are, however, a few stragglers. You see them in pairs, rounding corners, crossing streets like they know how walk-signals work. I once saw a couple of them sitting at a bus stop. Most of them are fairly timid, but there are two particularly frightening ones that refuse to submit to the neighborhood development, to the increase in traffic and to the crews of Animal Control agents that patrol the neighborhood doing whatever it is that they do.

These dogs, a filthy white Akita and a brown German Shepherd-ish looking one, usually hang out down on Chartres Street. If you take Chartres out of the French Quarter toward the Industrial Canal, it will lead you past blown-out warehouses, past the creepy brickyard with wooden crosses dangling from the fence, past the house inhabited by circus clowns that stinks of leaking sewage, past the compound that belongs to local folk-art mogul Dr. Bob, past the block that floods with every rain and is decorated with hand-painted sings warning, "SLOW— NO WAKE," past razor wire fences, houses falling down and houses being restored. Past all of that, a block before the tracks, you'll come to an intersection. On your right, there's the Mazant Street wharf and the river. On your left, a packing plant of some sort with a big parking lot and a stench of death so awful that it burns your nose and throat just to breathe. That's where they hang out.

They took us by surprise the first time we encountered them. My roommate, Desmond, and I were riding home leisurely after a show or something, taking our time and talking. He was in mid-sentence, saying something about how the smell of death wasn't so bad that night, when I caught a glimpse of a blur coming at us from behind. A fast, fluffy, snarling blur. A pair of blurs, actually.

"Ride!" I yelled as I realized what was happening. It took Desmond a moment to understand that I wasn't just trying to get away from the smell. That split-second hesitation had given me enough time to get about a quarter of a block ahead of him. I couldn't tell what was happening, but I could hear the dogs barking. They got very close to Desmond, but then we were over the railroad tracks and they let up. The barking continued, but I could hardly hear them over Desmond's hysterical laughter, which was soon joined by mine as well. We were still recapping the situation excitedly when we were safely inside our house.

Modern American society, with all of its conveniences, all of its ATMs, Stop n' Shops and drive-through cappuccino joints, has managed to suck most of the adventure right out of our lives, even down-and-out kids and stray dogs in New Orleans' Ninth Ward. I've always found it kind of sad that, through centuries of domestication and fascistic, forced in-breeding, all dog hunting instincts have been boiled down to little more than the urge to chase Frisbees, roll around in poop, and get really upset about the sound skateboard wheels make on pavement. Then it occurs to me that humans (Americans, I believe, in particular) have, through the installation of Stop n' Shops and whatnot, boiled our own hunter-gatherer instincts down to little more than getting really stoked when we get a good parking spot or find a really great coupon for our drive-through cappuccinos. Our lives, down to the routes we take to get places, what we eat, and what we do for fun, are more or less laid out by whatever society we exist in. There aren't really many adventures left anymore. I have yet to be convinced (despite the best efforts of SUV advertisements) that anything you have to purchase can really be considered "adventure." So people turn to drugs or shoplifting or driving SUVs or, in our broke and bored case, getting chased on road bikes down pothole-ridden Ninth Ward streets by big angry dogs that want to hurt us.

After that first frenzied chase sequence, I realized that the feeling of sheer terror had been missing from my life for some time. A couple of days later, while sitting around the house, feeling sorry for myself about whatever romantic or financial trouble I'd found myself in, I walked away from a small social gathering, grabbed my trusty pink bicycle and pedaled on over to Chartres Street. I rode a few blocks out of my way and looped around so that when the dogs took up chase I'd be headed back toward my house. The smell of death was particularly rank and was almost unbearable even before I'd reached the packing plant lot. I breathed through my mouth as I rode up slowly and looked around. There were a couple of Mack trucks with generators or something in them humming, but other than that there were no signs of life.

Oh well. Dumb idea anyway. I was just being dramatic. I should just get over whatever's bothering me. Suck it up, drive on. I'd just go home, hang out, act cheerful, try to be witty, maybe watch a movie I'd already seen like a million times — oop — never mind. The two shadows loped along on the side of one of the humming trucks, then they stepped out into the street light. They stopped when they saw me, just stood there, with their heads cocked, no doubt thinking: What does this guy think he's doing? Doesn't he know that there are a couple of *wild dogs* over here? Can't he see that we have important *wild dog business* to attend to?

I didn't have much time to wonder about what they'd been doing, though, before the big white one (always the leader of the pair) shot forward so suddenly that I nearly fell over backwards. The brown one followed suit and they were within about ten feet of me by the time I'd pointed my bike in the right direction and gotten myself moving. I was in too low of a gear as I headed up the incline toward the tracks and I couldn't get my right foot into its toe-clip, so the thin metal was scraping hard on the ground every time I pedaled. The white dog got so close to me that I was sure I would feel teeth latch onto my pants leg, and I was afraid I would have to kick him in the face to fend him off. My foot finally popped into the (now slightly bent) toe-clip properly and I shot over the railroad tracks. Both the dogs fell off, standing just behind the rails and barking at me, as they had the first time. Suddenly it was just me again, a kid on his bike, riding toward home. Perfectly normal.

Does everyone in New Orleans have these moments? Are wild dog attacks just par for the course of living in the Big Easy? Just like floods, giant cockroaches, 90% humidity levels, man-eating potholes and tourists? Or is it a phenomenon confined to the limits of the Ninth Ward? I'd guess that your average uptown investment banker probably doesn't get chased by any animals on his way home from the office. Even if he did he'd probably just mow them down in his SUV while bragging on his cell-phone to his mistress about the wonders of four-wheel drive. It might do average folks some good, being confronted with their own mortality in the form of a big, dirty, pissed-off pit bull. Who couldn't use that sort of life affirmation every now and then? Of course, it would probably become trendy just like fire walking and bungee jumping did, and, before you knew it, some entrepreneur would be on infomercials advertising his inspirational seminars to boost your self-esteem to the point where YOU TOO CAN HAVE THE CONFIDENCE IT TAKES TO GET CHASED THROUGH NEW ORLEANS BY ANGRY WILD DOGS!! Clubs would be erected and our run-down neighborhood would become a mecca for yuppies who can only relieve the stress and hardships of their six-figure jobs by being chased down by Genuine Wild Dogs. There'd be a big, multi-part special on *60 Minutes* or *20/20* and, after the big *Sports Illustrated* spread hit the newsstands, our two hometown dogs would probably be replaced by lean, mean, yuppie-chasing dogs specially bred in some lab somewhere. Fuck that! Better to keep my low-budget catharsis techniques to myself.

"Let's go!" said my roommates in unison when they found out what I'd been doing. I'd broken my vow of silence under the pressure of their brilliant interrogation strategy: asking me where I'd been. The three of us set out, on our way to the neighborhood bar with free pool via a short side trip to Wild Dog Land. Encouraged by our numbers, we took a side street, which met Chartres Street right by the doggy danger zone. When the duo saw us and took up chase, though, Colin steered his monster of a delivery basket at them and, apparently sensing no fear from him, they turned tail and fled back into the shadows of the stinky packing plant. Desmond and I stopped and dismounted our bikes beside Colin, but even with us just standing there they didn't come out. They didn't even bark.

"Gee, dude," Desmond said to Colin, "that wasn't very nice."

"Yeah," I added, "I think you broke their spirit."

Colin looked guilty. "I…I didn't mean to."

"Whatever, fucker," Desmond said, riding away in disgust.

We didn't see them for a while after that. I began to think they'd been ruined when Colin called their bluff. Maybe they thought that they were no good as wild dogs and now were living out some pathetic existence down by the Industrial Canal, eking by on the water-logged carcasses of wharf-dwelling Nutria rats. This theory, however, is not how reality works. I think that someone once told me that dogs are incapable of remembering specific incidents, just people, places and things. Everything else is just controlled by their instincts. Now that I think about it, though, I realize that the same guy who told me that also told me that if you drink six shots of espresso in under three minutes then your heart will explode and kill you, so I don't know why I'm giving any of that guy's fucked up facts any validity.

We were sitting on the stoop outside of our house. When we'd moved in, the steps said "Keep Off Steps" in large black letters, but now, through some skillful editing read, "Keep Off Hipsters." We were probably drinking beer or some equally idle activity when the dogs came bopping around the corner. They didn't see us at first and appeared to be searching for food outside the redneck bar across the street. Desmond thought that he would take this opportunity to befriend them, which he attempted by walking at them, hands out, Jesus-style, chanting, "Wild dogs, here wild doooogs, come on dogs" over and over in a spooky baby-talk voice. When the dogs spotted him, though, they just trotted off down the crumbling Ninth Ward sidewalk.

That, and one more sighting, made me realize that the poor critters weren't really vicious *or* broken, but were actually not that different from everyone else in our neighborhood. Desmond was driving me to my first day at a job I had no desire to have. I was late by the time we were passing the stinky death-lot. The smell wasn't so bad that afternoon and we spotted the dogs in the field across Mazant Street from where they normally were, lying in the grass near some playground equipment. The brown one was just lounging there, panting in the warm sunlight while the white one rolled around on its back, flailing its legs in the air doing that upside down "I've got an itch!" dance that dogs sometimes do.

"Wow," said Desmond as he slowed the car down to stare, "they aren't very scary when they're playing in the grass."

No sir, Desmond, they sure aren't. The poor bastards are just trying to get by, just like everyone. Hell, no one wants to be put on a leash. They're trying to hold their lives together in the neighborhood they call home, and they have their work cut out for them. "Progress" in the form of urban renewal and rising property values and, unfortunately, the presence of floundering white kids like myself, threaten them like it threatens a lot of the folks that have been here for a long time. While the people have skyrocketing rent to worry about, the dogs have to worry, too, about being netted and thrown in a van that says "New Orleans Animal Control" on the side. That kind of pressure would make anyone a little anti-social, wouldn't it?

UP LEE'S ASS

THE FIRST TIME I went into the tower was with G.K. during a dance party in the abandoned YMCA — the after-party for the Third Annual New Orleans Book Fair. During the day, the hotshots of the independent publishing world had come together to discuss the finer points of literature and the written word. As the day wore on, though, and more and more beer was consumed, their pretensions had fallen away along with their inhibitions. By afternoon it was just a big forum for trading copy shop scams. By nighttime, books were definitely in the back of these people's minds. The party was an apocalyptic version of a high school homecoming dance: DJ Karo had his generator-powered turntables set up underneath a banner with some generic revolutionary propaganda spray-painted across it; a bunch of punks and weirdoes were shaking it to Prince and Salt N' Pepa on the gymnasium floor while kids on bikes raced around the track above all of our heads. It should've been cathartic, seeing a bunch of my maniac friends reinventing the traumatic scenario of a school dance, but actually it was just causing all of my highschool era feelings of awkwardness and inadequacy to come bubbling back up, and I was hiding in the shadows on the bleachers, afraid that at any moment someone might sneak up and give me a wedgie or pants me.

G.K., shaking his ass below the bleachers, spotted me and yelled. I couldn't make out what he was saying, but it sounded suspiciously like, "Have you been up Lee's Ass?!" G.K had been drinking for about twelve hours, and I had no clue what he could possibly be going on about, but as he climbed up the bleachers to meet me, I was glad for the distraction.

"What?!" I yelled back, my face inches from his.

He motioned me toward the door. I grabbed a couple of beers from my bag and followed him. We wove our way through dancing revelers and past the worried-looking crowd that had just shown up, their eyes darting back and forth looking for some sliver of evidence that perhaps this wasn't *completely* illegal. G.K. stepped out of the building through a hole in the crumbling cinderblock wall that was serving as an entrance. I followed. Once in the relatively quiet parking lot, where a clump of crusties sat passing forties around and bitching about how they'd been misled into believing they were going to a party at a "real squat," I asked G.K. if he would kindly repeat himself.

"Have you been up Lee's ass?" he asked.

I tried to think of anything I'd ever done that might be described like that.

"Uhh ..." I said.

He finished off the dregs from his can of Bud, grabbed my jacket sleeve and exclaimed, "Well, c'mon!" leading me through the parking lot and up the block to Lee Circle, the big roundabout in the middle of the Central Business District. It must've been around three a.m., and the only signs of life were from the occasional cab rattling past us around the circle. We could hear the hum of traffic passing on the interstate, a block up and fifty feet above us.

I recalled other times G.K. had led me on drunken misadvenures, the most eventful of which was an aimless romp around the quarter that had ended with a guy pulling a gun on us because we didn't have any change to give him. As long as that doesn't happen again, I thought, everything will be fine.

We mounted the steps to the monument at Lee Circle. Eighty or so feet above us (later there would be heated debate and much pseudo-scientific hypothesizing on the exact height), atop a narrow concrete pedestal, stood the huge bronze figure of General Lee, staring out across his old stomping ground. We mounted the steps that led up the little hill at the base of the monument. There, as always, were a few homeless guys, curled up in sleeping bags and blankets, heads resting on duffle bags, protected from sight by the shrubbery that surrounded the towering monument.

G.K. crept past them to a big steel grate right by the base of the tower. I'd sat and drunk beers by that monument a dozen times without ever having paid the grate any mind. There was a padlocked latch on the edge of the grate, but when G.K. reached down and opened the thing, the whole latch came up, the bolts that had anchored it to the cement having already been ripped out.

"What the fuck are we doing?" I asked.

"Shhh!" warned G.K., looking around at the sleeping bodies and the non-existent traffic. "Just get in the fucking hole!"

I looked down at the darkness in the hole. I couldn't see what was down there, or how deep it was, but I could feel a sticky warmth wafting out at us and could smell the overwhelming odor of rank urine. In I went, making my way down a little ladder mounted to the side of the concrete hole. About three feet down I hit ground. G.K. followed me down and lowered the hatch behind us, so that we were stooped over just below it, our eyes adjusting slowly to the dark, my gag reflex rising up against the noxious smell.

"Gee, this is really great, G.K.," I whispered. "I'm glad we could do this together."

"Follow my voice," he said, and started to head deeper into the little cave. Soon we could stand up, and a few feet later we were in a tiny, round space. I could feel cool air above me and when I looked up I realized that we were in the hollowed out center of the tower. Somewhere, eighty or so feet above us, the bronze image of Robert E. Lee looked out over the city.

"Get up the ladder," G.K. said.

I looked at the ladder, and saw more steel rungs like the ones we'd just come down. A lot more. I'm not afraid of many things. Snakes don't bother me, nor do spiders or the dark or breaking into federal property. But when I was little, my two older brothers used to tie me up in a sleeping bag and pretend that they were going to throw me off of the roof. They wouldn't throw me off the roof, they'd open and shut windows and say, "Ok, we're on the roof now. We're heading to the edge. OK, now we're going to drop you. Bye!" And they'd drop me onto a bed or the couch. It didn't hurt me physically, but those split seconds in the air were terrifying enough to leave me permanently afraid of both heights and small, enclosed places. And the tower had both.

But my curiosity, tag-teaming with the seven or eight Schlitz's I'd had earlier, got the better of me. Up we went. One hand over another, me first, heading toward the tiny ball of light visible somewhere high above our heads. The climbing was difficult, but the height didn't bother me since I couldn't see. Also, I reasoned, if I fall, I'll just land on G.K., and judging by his muttering, he can't be more than four or five feet below me. I tried to look at him, but really couldn't see a thing. If I tried to look up to see how far away the opening was, I'd whack my forehead on the steel safety cage that surrounded the ladder. So, looking straight ahead at the barely visible wall, I kept going.

And kept going and kept going. Right when I thought my arms might give out, the air turned suddenly cool and (comparatively) fresh. I came into an opening and flopped onto the floor beside the ladder, pressing myself against the wall of the little room I was in. My Acrophobia kicked back in, getting me back for the climb, with interest.

G.K. followed. Drunker than I, and more confident from having done this before, he was immediately standing up in the tiny room, frightfully close to the dark hole we'd just come out of, looking around like someone surveying a newly purchased piece of land. "Really," he said, winded. "It's a pretty crappy view." And after a moment's thought added, "And I think this is illegal."

There were four windows in the room, looking out on the river, on downtown, on the interstate and toward the French Quarter. After a few minutes I forced my shaking legs to hoist me up and peeked out of the windows. The view was, as G.K. had pointed out, fairly unspectacular, just the roofs of warehouses and motels and part of the Mississippi River Bridge. But seeing the city I'd lived in for six years from a new vantage point, one I never would've thought existed, gave me hope.

See, things had been going bad for me in New Orleans. I was near to the point of abandoning ship, and I thought I'd done everything there was to do there: I'd marched in funeral parades; I'd worked practically every bike delivery job in the Quarter; I'd sat on the abandoned, collapsing wharf by the Mississippi; canoed through (and even swum in) Bayou St. John; spied on a pair of Nutria rats, the giant aquatic rats that are destroying the coastline, as they swam into the moonlight; drank whiskey in an abandoned water tower; wandered around in the swamp; gone to a museum or two; realized that I hate chicory in my coffee; and even been punched in the face by a guy who I'm pretty sure was a member of a world-famous, singing New Orleans family. But I'd never been up Lee's ass.

That was a good sign.

Part II

Things got worse and worse for me after that. I'd been staying with my girlfriend. We broke up and I moved into a sublet; the sub-letter came back to town and I had nowhere to go. Out of desperation, I moved into the lowest and most chaotic of all punk houses, *The House of Bad Starts*. The house, in the middle of the quickly developing (upper) Ninth Ward neighborhood, had recently been procured by Chloe and Buzz. They were traveling kids, the kind that lined the fronts of businesses on Decatur Street with their dogs, sparing change, playing toy accordions, and putting on baffling, garbled puppet shows with the random garbage they'd found.

Of the two, I knew Buzz better. Buzz had recently gotten a job at a hip coffee shop and, with her newly-found income, began amassing an enormous and wildly flamboyant wardrobe. With each paycheck, her height would increase an inch or two as she progressed, successfully, on the road to finding the biggest boots on the planet. She also began (or resumed perhaps, since I hadn't known her that long) to take copious amounts of speed. Before moving in with her, my interactions with Buzz usually went something like this: I'd be at the coffee shop putting soy milk in my maté or whatever, when she'd corner me, staring me down with huge, unblinking mascara-smeared eyes and saying things like, "Do you like my haircut? It's the first in a series of conceptual haircuts that I'm going to give myself."

"Whoah, yeah, Buzz, it's cool," I'd say, admiring the randomly-cropped patches of hair and skin. "What do you call it?"

"It's called…" she'd say, voguing her open hand around her head like a satellite in orbit, never taking her gaze off of me, "…*hospital*."

Another time I was sitting in the back of the café reading, when I heard Buzz clomping around the front room, sounding distressed. "I was fucking time robbed!" she yelled. "I was time robbed and now all of my CDs and my wallet are *gone*." I wasn't sure what "time robbery" was, and feeling inadequate about falling behind on punk vernacular, I asked a guy who was walking past toward the bathroom. He rolled his eyes and said, "I'm not sure. Maybe: 'I took too much drugs and can't remember anything.'"

"AAAh," I said, making a mental note. "Check."

Chloe was younger than Buzz, with something to prove. She played accordion, picked fights on the street, swigged pints of whiskey from paper bags, made puppets, dressed up like a China doll and had a spaced-out dog who ate underwear, and was named after some Egyptian god.

Chase lived there too, though he wasn't around much. Chase was an eighteen-year-old kid who was born and raised in New Orleans and had just moved out of his folks' house. He mostly worked and locked himself in his room, plotting his escape from the house.

The house itself was beautiful, a sprawling four bedroom place with unfinished trim, hardwood floors, weird little hallways that wrapped around curved rooms, a backyard and tool shed that was perfect for my increasingly large collection of power tools. The House of Bad Starts was owned by Mr. Jake, a local landlord famous throughout the Ninth Ward. Mr. Jake, who was pushing ninety, owned a couple handfuls of houses in the neighborhood, and still lived on his own. He was nearly blind and wiled away the days drinking pints of whiskey and telling rambling stories and fragments of philosophy to his visitors. Obviously, Mr. Jake wasn't the type to keep up on current market trends and property values, so his houses all fell under a sort of uneasy rent control thanks to the fact that his accounting didn't go past whether or not there was any Old Crow in the house. If there was, you wouldn't see Jake unless you went over to talk to him, to hear about his Mississippi childhood. If the whiskey ran out, Mr. Jake would go make his rounds, collecting rent from his various tenants around the neighborhood, none of whom he would've recognized out of the context of their front stoops.

I moved into the place in late summer, when the torrential downpours and virus-carrying mosquitoes descended on the city every day — the slow time, devoid of tourists, devoid of hipsters and punks, when all the people who actually live in New Orleans just putter around, fanning themselves with the Times-Picayune, drinking on their stoops. In The House of Bad Starts, no one was ever around. My room stayed cool, and I was paying eighty dollars a month for it. Those first few days were peaceful. I cooked food, started setting up my workshop in the shed, and painted my room a color that a neighbor described as "Fast Food Restaurant Orange."

This isn't so bad, I thought. I can handle this.

And then…summer was over. The dark clouds cleared up. The mosquitoes' tiny life spans ended, and tourists began to poke their Mardi-Gras-bead and Cat-in-the-Hat hat-clad heads out again. And with them came the punks. It's strange how punks claim to be isolated from society, yet in every hub of tourism, where capitalism and mainstream Americans are at their most concentrated and embarrassing forms, you'll find punks. They follow the bloated beast of consumerism around, eating its discarded pizza, drinking the beers it sets down on garbage cans so that it can catch more beads. Really, despite slogan-covered-patches that may claim otherwise, these punks are about as free from society's trappings as a tick is free of the dog. And New Orleans is possibly the most extreme example of this. Every year it seemed like every freight train in the country suddenly re-routed to New Orleans, dumping scores of kids in our town, all of them riding whatever was the newest wave of down-and-out homeless punk chic. Accordions and newsboy hats, overalls, fiddles, pit-bulls, washtub basses, Carhartt overalls, patches — everyone showing off their new face tattoos and staph infection scars, talking about the drug studies they were going to do, or how they were going to hop trains to Australia, or how this year, they were going to settle down, start that collective warehouse they've talked about ever since the already-existing collective warehouse in town kicked them out.

I was very aware of this New Orleans influx phenomenon, but it was usually easy enough to avoid these kids when I didn't want to be around dog fights and conversations about whether or not eating road-kill can be considered vegan. This year, though, I'd moved into ground zero. I came home one night from my job delivering po' boys and gumbo on my bicycle to a house completely full of traveling scumbags-in-training. It looked as though the entire cast of the Mad Max movies had been shot with some Scooby Doo-esque laser that turned them all into sixteen year olds. They lined the walls of the living room, each one clutching a plastic half-pint of Ancient Age blended whiskey, the whiskey-flavored grain alcohol that cost a buck eighty-five at the sketchy store around the corner. They were all screaming, playing instruments and letting their dogs run around (and shit) everywhere.

And it was going to be like this for a while. Every time I'd come home I'd cringe as I opened the door, horrified to find what new mania had descended upon the house while I was at work or the coffee shop or laundromat.

Here we go…I'd think as I would unlock the deadbolt, and then walk in to find that there was, suddenly, some tweaker who'd set up a tattoo shop outside my bedroom, giving face tattoos (and, it would later turn out, staph infections) to a waiting line of scumbags. Or there'd be kids fucking in the living room, yelling at me to close the goddamned door. Or, as happened one night when I came home from the bar, hoping I was drunk enough to sleep through the madness at home, Chloe down on her knees in the bathroom, X-ACTO knife in hand, dissecting a rat on a board.

"What are you doing Chloe?" I asked, trying to focus on the gore beneath her.

"I caught a rat and I'm going to tan its hide."

I looked at the poor rat, sliced open down its belly, innards glistening, its skin splayed out and nailed to the board.

"Huh," I said. "Can I pee in here?"

"Sure," she said, turning her attention back to her specimen. I peed and went to bed.

It got to the point where I couldn't make myself go home. I'd bike around endlessly, hang out at bookstores reading books I'd read before; at parties I'd be the last to leave, trying to get exhausted, already-drunk people to stay up just a little bit longer with me.

"C'mon, let's go dumpster-dive pizza and slingshot bottles by the river," I'd plead. I'd go to bars, or people's houses, and try to find friendly faces. Then I'd try to convince them to go to the tower with me.

Part III

"What do you think would happen if you fell?"

"You'd probably get lodged in the ladder."

"You think it would kill you?"

"I bet not at first. You'd just break your neck or collarbone, then stay in here screaming until you bled to death or died of thirst."

"Why the hell is it here, you think?"

"The windows angle out like a gun turret, so you can fire out at any angle but no one can fire in."

"Maybe the architect was planning for the day when he just lost it and came up here to pick off businessmen."

"Say you *were* to start shooting at people from up here…what do you think the cops would do?"

"Well…they'd probably blow it up with you in it, but first they'd probably just shoot at it for a few days."

"Oh I don't know. It seems like a sharpshooter on the roof of that hotel might be able to get a shot in here, then it would ricochet around until it hit you."

"Hmm. Yeah, maybe. Or if someone could make it up to the base of the monument they could throw a bunch of tear gas in there and try to gas you out that way."

"Huh. Yeah. It only took 'em a day to get Mark Essex off of the Howard Johnson. They used a helicopter."

"Yeah, but he was out in the open."

"Huh. Yeah."

I began going to the tower every day, sometimes twice a day. I pictured myself as the host of some demented talk show with the people I took up Lee's ass as my guests. I wouldn't really tell people where we were going until we were standing above the hatch, then I'd push them through and get them up the ladder in the same way G.K. had when I'd first come there. We'd sit up there, discuss, you know, how weird it was up there, and drink beers, sending the empties clattering down the rungs of the ladder into a quickly-growing pile. The rule I'd made with myself is that no matter how tempting it was, I would never go there alone, in case a drunken misstep sent me down the hole. So I'd take whomever I could, and warn them sternly, after they caught their breath and the shock of being in there wore off: "DON'T TELL ANYONE ABOUT THIS."

And then, one day, I got to the tower only to find that the welds on the hatch had been fixed, sealed up tight.

PART IV

One night I stopped by Dan and Morgan's house. They were college kids, these guys I knew from the little Midwestern town where I used to live. It was weird. They'd moved to New Orleans, for some reason, from the heartland and managed to move into the one house in our neighborhood that wasn't bright purple or lime green, wasn't a shotgun or wasn't equipped with a

Mardi-Gras-bead-covered balcony. It was a simple, Midwestern-looking house, built from a fifties Sears Roebuck plan, totally all-America, as though they'd brought it down with them.

Their connection to New Orleans was as mysterious as the house's nondescript appearance, and its normality reflected their own. They were just some dudes. Dudes who drank beer, listened to avant-garde rock, worked, and ate hamburgers. Pretty typical. And that was what I was looking for in a house then. Normal. I wanted to live with the most non-speed-snorting, not-rat-skinning homebodies I could find.

"Dude!" said Dan as he opened the screen door. "What's up, man?"

"Nothing," I said. "I just happened to be in the neighborhood. Thought I'd stop in."

"Cool, bro!" said Dan in his permanently excited way. "Want a beer?"

Dan was a funny guy to talk to. He was one of those people that would frequently say things twice, like "cool, cool" or "yeah, yeah!" and nod, as though he was listening to some really grooving funk band that no one else could hear. All the while, his lanky frame moved around excitedly, like those huge inflatable, dancing windsocks that they hook up to air compressors and put out in front of auto dealerships. It was kind of like hanging out with a cartoon character. In fact, Dan did all he could to make his life more cartoonish, he drew faces and superheroes on everything and usually had his shaggy blond hair tucked up into a bright orange ball-cap that had big woody the woodpecker eyes staring down at you.

"Is it too much," he once asked me, "to demand smiley faces and googly eyes on everything?"

I accepted the beer, and we made our way through the sparsely furnished living room into the kitchen. Under the fluorescent lights, Dan handed me a can of Miller that was left over from a show they'd had in their garage. We sat and chatted, talking about the little Midwestern town where we both, strangely, used to live.

"Man," he said, "I remember your old house. Every time I went by there, there'd be something crazy happening, and garbage everywhere, and like, people blowing fire and stuff."

"Oh yeah," I said. "We set the tree out front on fire that way."

"That place was fucked up."

"You should see the house I live in now," I told him.

Then conversation turned to work. I told him about my last job, doing bicycle delivery at a greasy sandwich place in the back of a French Quarter bar that had, listed on the menu, "Fried Twinkies."

"Man," said Dan, opening another can of Miller, "I should get a delivery job. Just gotta get a basket for that bike." He pointed a finger through the open door to the garage where his bike was leaning, an ancient three-speed Murray that I'd helped him work on many times.

"I have an extra basket," I told him.

"Yeah?"

"Yeah we can go over to my house and get it right now if you want."

"Okay, cool, cool."

"Just let me pee," I said. "Where's your bathroom again?"

"Top of the stairs. The light's behind the door."

"Cool."

I mounted the stairs and used the bathroom. As I came out, I noticed a little door on the wall opposite the bathroom door. When I reached up and opened it, I found myself looking into a big, empty attic, almost as big as my bedroom, with a window and everything.

A few minutes later we were pulling up in front of The House of Bad Starts, where a bunch of kids were crouched on the stoop, screaming about Dungeons and Dragons characters.

"No way could your ork take out my wizard with only four fire power!"

a kid with a padlock through his nose was saying.

We stepped over them, made our way across the trash-strewn floor of the house, through the kitchen, into the room where the ad-hoc tattoo shop had been set up. Dan tried to stay calm, keeping his eyes (and, in effect, the cartoon googly eyes on his hat) trained on the floor directly in front of where he was walking. But I could tell he was a bit un-nerved by the cluster of dubious characters in the room. They were standing around watching a girl about to get roses tattooed on her forehead while Seth, the tweaker tattoo artist, stumbled around wildly going, "I know I had those needles somewhere."

I undid the bulky padlock on my bedroom door and fetched the basket for Dan. We attached it to his bike outside, up the sidewalk from where the ork and the elf were arguing.

"Alright man, thanks, thanks," Dan said, bobbing his head, no doubt stoked to be moments away from leaving the house.

"Sure, no problem, Dan," I said, gathering my wrenches from the ground and hitting the basket with my palm to test its sturdiness.

"Well, I'll see you later," he said, mounting the old Murray.

"Yeah, for sure," I said. Then, trying to sound as though it hadn't been in the front of my mind all night, added, "Hey Dan, have you ever thought about renting out y'all's attic?"

"The attic? Shit…I guess it would make a pretty sweet room, huh?"

"Yeah, if you and Morgan were into it, I'd rent it for a couple hundred bucks or something."

"Alright, man, I'll talk to Morgan."

"Yeah that'd be awesome."

"Don't worry," he said. "We'll get you out of this place, Ethan."

"Thanks, Dan."

"Cool, cool."

PART V
Memorable conversations from The House of Bad Starts:

"You see that kid?"

"Which one?"

"The one passed out on the Hide-a-Bed."

"Yeah."

"This morning he was reading on the couch and he looked up and said, 'Well guys, I just shat myself.' Then walked out of the room. Just like that. Totally calm."

"Whoah …"

"Yeah."

* * *

"I just had a conversation with a very reasonable neighbor of yours who says someone tagged his house. He's extremely angry and thinks that it was someone staying here."

"It probably was. Which neighbor was it?"

"It was the man who lives in the house up the street that is painted like a huge American flag."

"What did he say he wanted to do to the person, call the cops?"

"No, he said that he was going to kill them."

"So the guy lives in a house that is painted like a huge American flag and is looking to kill someone for writing on said house?"

"Right."

"This is obviously some connotation of the term 'very reasonable' that I was not previously familiar with. Do you know who wrote on his house?"

"I do."

"Does this person remember writing on the house?"

"No."

"Oh. Good. Just don't tell them they did it."
"OK."
"OK."

* * *

"Hey, do you like sauerkraut?"
"What?"
"Do you like sauerkraut?"
"Uh…yeah."
"Good, I was just about to make sauerkraut. You can have some of it."
"Who the fuck are you?"
"What?"
"Who are you? Why are you in my house? Do you know anyone that lives here?"
"You don't need to talk to me this way."
"Get out of my house!"

* * *

"Hey, quit!"
"Uh…what?"
"Quit fucking punching him!"
"Stay out of this, man. You don't know what he did."
"I don't give a shit what he *did*. He's crying and you're punching him in the face in my flowerbed."
"I…I shouldn't be standing in your flowerbed. I'm sorry."

* * *

"Hello?"
"Hey Ethan, it's Dan."

"Hey Dan. How's it going?"

"It's going alright. How you doing man?"

"I just had to stop some dude from punching a hundred-pound kid in the face in my flowerbed, but other than that, you know, not bad."

"Cool, cool. Look man, I talked to Morgan about, you know, the attic and stuff?"

"Yeah?"

"Yeah. He's down, man, you know what I'm saying?"

"Yeah? You think I could move my stuff in pretty soon?"

"Yeah man, I think so."

"Okay, how about in like…twenty minutes?"

"Alright man, alright."

"See you then."

"Bye."

"Bye."

PART VI

So for the fifth time in a year, I packed up my tools and my records, my books and my zines, and my nervous little dog; I took down my increasingly ragged show flyers and band posters, and I loaded them all up into my antiquated yellow Dodge Maxi Van, and I moved again. I don't even remember if I informed anyone at The House of Bad Starts of my sortie. And I don't know if they even noticed.

My attic-room at the new house, which had no punk name, was like a little tree house, all bare wood and slanted ceilings. Had it not been for the asbestos-covered pipe in the middle of the room and the blown insulation everwhere, it might've been considered "quaint."

I'd moved in so quickly that Dan and Morgan's friends had no idea that anyone was living in there and occasionally when I came bounding out of the little elevated door, I would frighten some collegiate artsy type who was just looking for the bathroom.

I built a loft, and I screwed egg crates to the wall to put my clothes in. I stuffed all the ancient, filthy insulation back into the far regions of the attic and sealed those parts off with scraps of found plywood. I wrapped fabric around the asbestos-covered pipe to keep myself from brushing up against it but also to, you know, liven the place up a little bit.

Dan didn't find a delivery job, but I found a new one, at the infamous Bastille Marte, the place where drunks could stumble in for hot sausage po' boys at any time of the day; the place where you could drink outside as long as you didn't disturb the neighbors; the place that once served a cigarette butt in an order of chicken parmesan. I'd spend days delivering gumbo to parking lot attendants, twice-baked potatoes to bellhops, catfish to tourists. At night, it'd be sandwiches to strippers, burgers to bartenders, and all kinds of stuff to that house over on Royal where they made the hardcore gay porn. Then I'd go home to my wooden room in the air, drink fancy beers paid for by tips, and try to figure out what to do with my life.

PART VII

Moira showed up in town one day. We'd lived together seven years before and hadn't seen each other since. When we'd parted ways she had been an artsy bike messenger in Philadelphia. She'd moved there from San Francisco with her boyfriend Toby and spent her days drawing pictures, painting graffiti, and stenciling vague, threatening messages on her clothing. I had been a seventeen-year-old runaway who chain-smoked Marlboros, shoplifted everything, lived on Mountain Dew and White Castle hamburgers, and would sleep until dusk every day. Then, upon hearing Moira or Toby come home from work, would jump up and pretend like I'd been doing something really productive.

When I ran into Moira at a café in New Orleans, I barely recognized her from beneath the layers of dirt, the patched-up Slayer shirt and mass of dreadlocks that hung over her face. She'd been living in Alaska where she worked as a welder at a dry-dock. New Orleans was, by some logic that was never clear to me, her mid-point on a trip from Anchorage to Mexico. She was hanging out for a while, waiting on friends.

We hugged and spent the rest of the day reminiscing and catching up, talking about our fucked up, graffiti-covered house in South Philly.

"You really grew up," she said, comparing twenty-five-year-old me with seventeen-year-old me. "Man …" she added, squinting as her mental image of seventeen-year-old me came into sharper focus. "You were really annoying! And I don't think you ever gave us any rent at all."

"I gave y'all twenty bucks once," I said.

"Really?" she said. "I don't remember that."

"Yeah! I totally gave you twenty bucks! I shoplifted a bunch of sailing supplies for this weird guy and he paid me like sixty bucks. I think I spent the rest on White Castle hamburgers or something."

I invited Moira over to the Midwestern oasis. I introduced her to Dan and Morgan and they struck up an uneasy acquaintance. Dan and her discussed drawing and graffiti. I think Morgan hid in his room, and she moved into our living room for a while. It was the least I could do after she'd let me squat her apartment seven years prior.

Soon it was like the old days. We rode around all day, worked on bikes in the backyard, drew cartoons, got drunk, and plotted crimes. One night, on a bike ride around the Central Business District, we rode by the tower. I told her about the little room at the top.

"Whoah. I wish we could get in," she said.

We went up and tried the hatch, but with no luck; there were three or four sloppy welds around the edges. We yanked on it hopefully, accomplishing nothing but annoying the guys sleeping by the hedge around us, who made a show of fluffing their make-shift pillows and rolling over in a huff.

"Dammit," I said peering up at my prior hangout.

"A torch would get us in," said Moira, eyeing the plate steel hatch.

PART VIII

"What do you want this stuff for?" Mutt asked as we loaded his portable welding setup into my big hiking pack. Moira and I both stammered, eyeing each other. Mutt rolled his eyes. "Never mind," he said. "Don't tell me. Just don't get my shit confiscated, goddammit."

"Deal," I said. "Thanks, Mutt."

"Yeah," he said, stuffing his huge dreadlocks under a cap and leading us through his apartment past heaps of tools, motorcycle parts, sleeping punk rockers and beer bottles. "Just get my tanks back to me."

We put the heavy pack full of equipment into the basket of my old red Schwinn and wheeled down Press Street to my house. In the garage, I gathered wrenches, regulators and a cutting torch borrowed from another friend. Dan and Moira folded up the huge banner we'd been working on, the letters painted with thick coats of house paint that still hadn't entirely dried. The banner was painted on tablecloths that we'd swiped from a fancy hotel downtown in whatever colors we could find. The message was political, rather uninspired, but so chosen because of the clear view of the tower from the freeway. "OIL=WAR" it read in red. Then spelled out by the shapes of stick figure bodies: "1184 DEAD" (which was the U.S. death count in Iraq at the time).

Moira, Dan and I set out toward the sealed tower, the oxy-acetylene equipment in Dan's basket, the banner in mine.

"I will admit that I am slightly nervous about all this!" I confessed to Dan on the ride toward downtown.

"Ethan," he said, "We're going to cut into a state monument using

FIRE, then drop a political banner down the side of it. What could possibly go wrong?"

I looked at him for a long time as we rode side by side. The googly eyes on his ball cap stared back at me. "I don't know what to say to that," I replied.

We headed through the New Orleans Central Business District. Besides the few random bars that were too dark to see inside (and that I'd never heard of anyone actually stepping into), there was no life down there. We crossed the treacherous trolley tracks, which can spell doom for the unaware cyclist, and our target came into view. Lee's ass.

Just then, another cyclist, the only one we'd passed since leaving the house, an old guy on a squeaky cruiser, came coasting around the corner in a wide, drunken arc. He was headed the wrong way down St. Charles Avenue, straight toward us. More precisely, straight toward Dan and the veritable bomb that he had hidden away inside the backpack in his basket. As the gap between them closed, my grip on my handlebars stiffened. The old guy seemed oblivious to the impending crash, and was definitely oblivious to the full weight of the situation. Dan tried to swerve, but as he did, the other guy tried to as well, putting them back on the same path toward one another. They did this again, and again. Moira and I both screamed something inarticulate at the same time, and then Dan and the drunk dude finally got it right and circumvented one another at the last moment.

"Damn," muttered the guy as he continued on his way. "Chill, white people!"

"Yeah, really!" Dan (quite white himself) snapped, followed by a little "whew!" of relief.

We locked our bikes at the usual place, and while Dan and Moira carried the gear up the mound to the tower, I headed over to the Shell station to pick up our alibi: a six pack of tall-boys. This is one of the beautiful things about life in New Orleans. Drinking in public is legal, encouraged even, and the phrase "we're just drinking a few beers, officer" is a legitimate excuse for being somewhere totally suspicious. Or so we hoped, at least, as back at the monument we piled our bikes in front of the hatch and cracked the tall-boys, me and Dan hoping to obscure any passing cops' view of Moira, who had found a cardboard box that she was proceeding to do her work underneath. With a crescent wrench she attached the regulators to the tanks and opened them, first oxygen, then acetylene. She sparked the striker in front of the torch and with a loud "Foomp!" the flame burst from the beak-like tip of the tool. Moira pulled a pair of tinted goggles over her eyes and kneeled down behind the box.

"Can you see me?" she asked from beneath it.

"No," I said, looking at her. A cab rolled by without paying us any mind. "You're good. It just looks like a box."

"Cool." Then she hit the lever on the torch that increases the oxygen and makes the flame appropriate for cutting. It made a loud hissing noise and suddenly the whole tower was cast in a bright blue light with a tall shadow going up it that looked an awful lot like a small dreadlocked woman holding a cutting torch.

"Oh shit," said Dan, pulling his cap down over his eyes as though it would make us any more discreet. "You gotta be kidding me!"

I was trying to think of exactly what we might say when the cops arrived at the scene, wondering if "What seems to be the problem, officer?" would be appropriate when suddenly the bushes just in front of where we were sitting began to rustle.

"What the hell?" I muttered.

A long-haired kid in his early twenties, sleepy-eyed and dirty, popped up from the bushes. He was shirtless but wore a leather jacket and a sleeping bag draped around his shoulders.

"What are you fucking doing, man?" he asked, rubbing his eyes.

The blue light suddenly vanished and Moira popped her head up from under the box.

"Something's wrong with this torch," she said, removing her goggles and blinking fiercely.

"Us?" I said in response to the kid whose rest we had so rudely interrupted. "I, uh…well, we're trying to cut our way into this monument with a welding torch. What are you doing?"

His eyes widened as he grasped the weight of the situation.

"Oh, *hell* no!" he exclaimed, quickly trying to shove his few belongings into a backpack. "Oh, no way man, I just got into this town. You're not getting my ass arrested," he was saying, panicky, trying to find everything. He tossed his shoes out of the bush onto the plot of concrete that we were sitting on and clumsily tried to get them around his bare feet. "I mean," he continued, "You're fucking with the south! You're fucking with the OLD South!"

He finally got his shoes on and zipped his pack. Meanwhile, Moira had adjusted the levels on the torch and relit it, the wavering light once again projecting her huddled shape onto the tower beneath where old General Lee held his stoic vigil.

"How can we get this guy to stay and help block Moira from the road?" I thought as the freaked-out squatter began to make his way down the steps away from us, still muttering to himself about the atrocity of our crimes.

"Hey, you want a beer?" I asked. He stopped cold, and turned slowly, perhaps anticipating some sort of treachery but finding me smiling sincerely, holding out one of the over-priced tall cans of Busch that I had procured from the Shell.

"Yeah, alright," he said, dropping his pack and plopping down beside us and our bikes. "It's fucked up what happened in Ohio," he added, opening his can and seemingly forgetting about the threat of arrest.

"Hey, Ethan," Moira said, still having logistical issues with the torch. "Can you check this out?"

I crawled around to the opening of the box and began helping her adjust the thing. Both of the regulators were broken, so we just had to guess at the gas levels and the flame kept jumping and not remaining regular, making it impossible to get the right type of flame for cutting. As we struggled with it, Dan made conversation with our guest.

"What happened in Ohio?" Dan asked him.

"Man," said the kid, sputtering, obviously flabbergasted that Dan didn't even know. "They killed Dimebag, man!"

"Oh yeah," Dan said. "That sucks." He was referring, apparently, to the ex-guitar player of southern-fried heavy metal heroes Pantera (whom I actually had ties to through my sometime-employer, The House of Shock Haunted House, but that is definitely a different story). Dimebag had been gunned down onstage by some random maniac (and not, to the best of my knowledge, by any shadowy group as was implied by our bush-dwelling compatriot's conspiratorial use of "they").

"Try it again," I said, having tried my hand at adjusting the torch. Moira hit the oxygen lever, and the flame turned a bright blue again, right in front of my unshielded face, leaving me blinded by blobby red spots in my eyes. I stood to get away from the flame and took one step into what felt like nothing at all.

"Holy shit!" I heard Dan shout as I fell forward. I jerked back on my other leg, still planted on the ground, and somehow, amazingly regained stability. My vision cleared and I was left looking into a manhole that, had I fallen into it, would've no doubt left me with at least a broken hip.

This was all the young, metal-head traveler could bear. He slammed the remainder of his beer and blurted something like "Have a good night." He trotted off to find somewhere safer to sleep: the median of the interstate, perhaps, or inside a bear cage at the zoo.

I too had had enough. "Come on, this isn't working. I say we cut our losses and try to figure out what's wrong back at the house."

My friends agreed. We packed up, finished our beers and left. The only damage we'd done was a small, bubbly, molten spot on the hatch, and possibly a dent to the mental well-being of that bush-dwelling metal head.

PART IX

We did drop the banner, eventually, in a far less dramatic setting. It was an abandoned parking garage a block away from the tower. The thrill was gone already, however, our adrenal glands having been sapped that night at the tower. When the deed was actually done, it was performed dogmatically like, "Well, we have this ninety-foot anti-war banner, guess we'd better throw it off of something." It didn't go so well, either. We never bothered to measure the parking garage, which turned out to be far shorter than Lee's tower, so the bottom of the banner just fell in a heap on the ground. Seeing this, I thought it might be too easy for someone to pull the banner down from the ground, so I hacked it in half, sawing at it from the second story with my pocketknife. When Dan, Moira and I regrouped on our bikes out on the street and viewed our work, we saw that my handy-work had edited our message slightly and the banner now read:

"OIL=WAR 1184 DEA"

"Well, that's cryptic," I said.

Exhausted, we rode home, past Robert E. Lee's eternal gaze, which, in the pale twilight of dawn, seemed to be mocking us in our bittersweet victory. By the time I'd gotten a few hours sleep and ridden back over to the garage, the banner had been discovered and removed.

PART X

Living with Dan and Morgan in the vinyl-sided house of normality was a definite improvement over The House of Bad Starts, but after several years of living in New Orleans, I felt it had done its damage on me. I woke up one day and realized, as though the scales had fallen from my eyes, that the local microbrew was expensive and tasted like rotten socks. I realized that the french fry po' boy, a sandwich made of french-fries, withered vegetables and a death-defying amount of mayonnaise (and frequently the only vegetarian item available at local eateries) and served on stale bread, isn't really even food, much less good food. I realized that I didn't want to live in a place where my dog could possibly be eaten by an alligator.

I made hasty plans to leave. Seeing as I was freshly unemployed and that I lived in someone's attic, this wasn't too difficult an undertaking. Soon my wheezing, older-than-I Dodge Maxi Van was packed full of my belongings. My dog was knowingly panicking at the prospect of moving for the sixth time in a year and exacting his revenge by peeing everywhere. I was ready to go, with the almost randomly-chosen destination of Asheville, North Carolina, a place that I'd visited twice and held a sun-soaked vision of, picturing it as the anti-New Orleans, as different as a place could be and still be in the same region. Beyond that, I wasn't sure what was waiting for me. I had about three vague acquaintances there, who I didn't even bother to call.

My last night in town was spent with a handful of friends drinking enough beer that I now haven't the foggiest idea of what we did. Somehow, though, our exploits led us uptown and right by Lee's Tower. We stopped and stared up at it. Taylor was there, the only one of our group of four who had been inside the tower with me. We were regaling the others with stories and jokes about the place, and we made our way up to where the hatch was. As I pointed out the little scabby spot where Moira had attempted our forced-entry a couple of weeks prior, I noticed something odd: All but two of the thick welds that held the hatch shut had somehow broken. The four of us hooked our fingers under one edge of the hatch, and, on three, pulled with all of our force. The thick steel hatch bowed up a little bit and with a loud "crack!" flew open, sending us all staggering drunkenly backward toward the hedgerow and the guys sleeping beneath it. I think three of us, including myself, cut ourselves. Even though I was bleeding from the wrist, I was excited, and quickly ran across the street to the Shell station to get more beer for my final climb up Lee's ass before I left town.

And we did it. We stumbled through the dark, urine-stinking crawl space. Whatever civil servants had welded the monument shut hadn't been made to clean our beer cans up, apparently, and we waded through them. We made the long, dark, knuckle-wrenching climb up the ladder. I probably bonked my head on that damn safety cage that surrounded the ladder, no doubt in the just-healed spot where I'd bonked it every single time I climbed the thing. We flopped out of the vertical tunnel, wheezing, into the tiny, pigeon-desecrated gun-turret, and I looked out over the city that I'd given nearly six years of my life to. There was the bridge that I had first driven in on, which I had accidentally gone too far on, thus ending up in the suburbs and having to pay a toll to get back to the city. (Damn New Orleans, I know they set that up confusingly on purpose.) There was the Shell Corporation building that I had worked across the street from as a barista, being forced to wait on Shell's coffee-drinking cubicle dwellers who had no control over their own lives except when it came to bossing me around during their breaks. There was the French Quarter, where I'd logged countless long hours biking around with greasy food in my basket, delivering it to the strippers and tourists and garage attendants. Just beyond that, with buildings too low to the ground to see, was our neighborhood, the Ninth Ward, where I'd lived in various vehicles and ramshackle houses, where my nervous Chihuahua and wheezing yellow Dodge were, at that moment, waiting to leave in the morning.

The next time I would see the city it was after it had just gotten its ass kicked by Hurricane Katrina, and everything would be different. At that time, though, standing in Lee's tower, it was me that had had my ass kicked by the city. By every failed friendship and love affair, every poor-tipping job, every tire-popping pothole. But I hadn't had it as bad as some. I'd only been arrested and put in New Orleans' notorious Orleans Parish Prison once, and was lucky enough to have friends to get me out quickly. I'd never been mugged or jumped like so many of my friends. These small bits of luck meant that it was time to quit while I was ahead. But standing there, in that tiny secret room, with our tiny secret view in four different directions, it didn't feel like time to go. It didn't feel like New Orleans was the menacing creature I had built it up to be in my mind. I thought over everything that my friends and I had worked for. We'd started non-profit organizations from nothing that turned people on to new ideas, and taught them how to fix bikes and how to read; we'd clogged the streets of the French Quarter with unsanctioned parades, celebrating life and our ability to create, to fill the darkness with our drumming and screams; we'd turned abandoned buildings into art galleries; we'd danced on rooftops and atop cars and along the riverbank late at night. It felt like, there, where no one could see us (though we could easily pick several pedestrians off with an assault rifle if we ever so chose), the city down there belonged to us. It was like some ant farm that we looked over, knowing we could shake it up whenever we wanted. I wouldn't miss the deeply imbedded problems of the city. I wouldn't miss the racism, the greed and power plays that the old money aristocrats used to keep the working class down and property values up. I wouldn't miss the constant threat of violence, or the leaky roofs or drunken tourists.

But I was going to miss shaking things up in a way that can only happen in that city. I was going to miss fucking with the south, fucking with the *old* south.

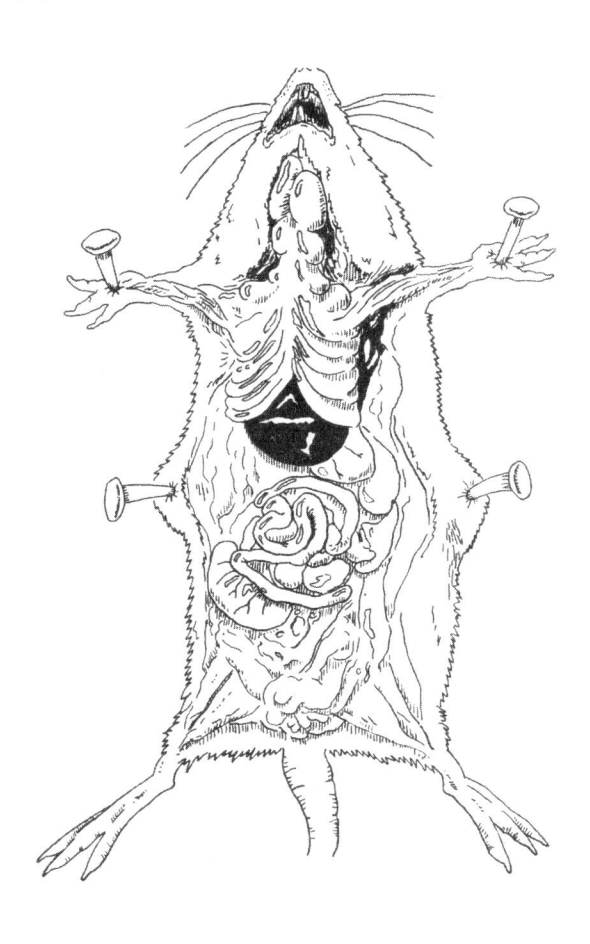

SCENES FROM A SHATTERED MEMORY OF NEW ORLEANS

1. Seeds Are Planted

I'd been to New Orleans a million times with my parents when growing up in Jackson, Mississippi. It was the closest "real city," the place where kids snuck off to when they had their parents' cars and a strong excuse. It was where I could find the spiky bracelets and band t-shirts with which I littered my existence. It was where, once, I stood on the corner of Jackson Square, next to the plot of grass where all the punks and scumbags hung out, known as Hippy Hill, which would soon be paved over and replaced with a more tourist friendly amphitheatre. I was with my mother, whose eyes were beginning to glaze over from heat and shopping. She held her bags of art and clothes at her side, perhaps wiped the dregs of powdered sugar from her lips, leftovers from the beignets we'd just eaten. As we waited for the traffic signal to change, we stood next to a guy around twenty. I was fourteen, a late-in-the-game Sex Pistols casualty who stuck safety pins through my ears whenever I was away from my parents' watch. The guy we stood next to (despite my mother's obvious mental efforts to teleport herself away from his proximity) was eating a po' boy out of the garbage. He had big blond dreadlocks that hung over his face, leaving only his pierced lips exposed. He had tattered black clothes and a pair of Chuck Taylor All-Stars.

"Spare some change?" he asked.

My mother shook her head "*no.*" Her instant-Southern-politeness smile appeared on her face (her knee jerk reaction to anyone that she didn't want to be around, and if put in front of a firing squad, my mother would probably go out with that smile) but her eyes stayed fixed on the orange "Don't Walk" signal.

"It sure would be nice not to have to eat out of the trash," the guy said, one blue eye peeking out from his ropes of hair.

"Not today," said my mom, her mind already honing in on her next purchase.

The signal changed. We crossed the street, and I thought, Damn…that guy looked cool.

Perhaps that's when things started going awry for me.

2. Crash Landing

I moved to New Orleans with Haley, my girlfriend at the time. We had nothing to our names except a minivan I'd bought in Mississippi, which broke down halfway there. We left the van, still smoking, in the hands of four teenagers, probably not even old enough to drive. I signed the title over to the only one of them that could write, and the last we saw of them they were pushing the big maroon beast, which I had bought less than twenty-four hours earlier, up the main street of a town called Magnolia. I stuck out my thumb and, with the help of a tow truck driver, a cop who made a big show of the fact that he listened to the alternative rock station, and a middle-class guy headed to the casinos, we rolled into our new home at dusk.

A few hours later we found the only people we knew in town, some vague acquaintances met here and there around the country. They were all in a crowded bar watching the Morning 40 Federation. Everyone in the audience was completely naked, drunk and dancing. Two days earlier we'd been in Iowa City, Iowa, where the wildest thing that ever happened was that, if you played your cards right, you'd get your ass kicked by frat boys. Nine hundred miles later, though, and we were suddenly in a room full of naked people dancing to a cacophonous brass band whose singer yelled songs about beer through a megaphone. It was too much. Haley and I stepped out onto the French Quarter sidewalk to try and get our heads straight.

A cop, on foot, approached us and said, "Y'all can't be blocking the sidewalk like this. You're gonna have to get back in the bar." Being eighteen years old at the time, Haley and I had never been kicked out of a bar before, much less into one.

3. Climate

It rained for thirteen days, *every* day, one summer. Not a little bit of rain, but a torrential downpour. Every day. I was living in a van (not the exploded one, but a Dodge conversion van inherited from my late grandfather) with my dog, Iggy, and every day I would get up and ride to work at six in the morning at a coffee shop in the Central Business District. My glasses would fog up and I'd navigate by the lit-up signs of businesses I recognized.

The parking garage by the Square, I'd think. I must be on Chartres Street. The Best Western…okay, only one more block to go.

The city, being below sea level, had unusual issues with pressure and drainage, and the manholes would overflow, bouncing their hundred pound covers around the way quarters do after you flip them. I'd get to work soaked through, change into dry clothes, drying my wet ones in the back room by the stereo that constantly played smooth jazz. At the end of my shift, which consisted of four hours of abuse from the latte-sipping middle-management types who came over from the Shell office, I would gather up my clothes, almost dry, and bike home, to the van, to walk my dog through the torrents. My van was covered in clothes in various stages of drying.

One day as I ventured to the library just trying to stave off my cabin fever, I ran into Otis. We were both biking, covered in ponchos. We looked like monsters.

"Where you staying?" Otis yelled over the sound of an undrainable city trying to drain itself. Our feet got completely submerged with every pedal and the chains of our bikes squeaked; trying to keep them oiled through this was futile.

"In my van!" I yelled back. "It sucks!"

"Shit, you should consider yourself lucky," he said, "because it's impossible for a van to leak as much as my house does!"

4. Chaos As Usual

After an abortive move back to Iowa City, Haley and I returned to New Orleans on Lundi Gras one night, in yet another minivan that we'd bought. We wove through crazy carnival traffic, with WWOZ blasting "Aiko Aiko." We'd finally figured out the poorly marked highway system, figured out how to get into town without crossing the Mississippi River Bridge, which it then costs a dollar to come back over. That's how they get you. But not us; we'd paid our dues. An hour later we were down on the street, just in time for the infamous Krewe du Poux parade to make its way to its point of terminus, Frenchmen and Chartres (pronounced "Charters" — New Orleans has one of the highest illiteracy rates in the country, a dubious title that they have retained in part by naming all the streets with French names that are then mispronounced. Just ask anyone who lived in the Calliope Street Projects, pronounced, "Cowlly-ope"). As it does every year, the parade had gone around the corner, picking up more and more punks, freaks, fire breathers, clowns, drummers, giant puppets and random maniacs until it flooded the street in front of Café Brazil, all of the bodies coming together into one entity, one throbbing, pulsing, drunken squid that wrapped its gaudy, colored tentacles around everything in its path.

Tensions had run high for the past couple Krewe Du Poux parades. In 1999 the cops had swooped in when revelers set fires in the street and the night ended in violence and bloodshed. It had been two years, but everyone still kept that threat of possible violence in the back of their minds. So late that night, after hours of partying without incident, when a sound like a gunshot shattered the steady roar of the festivities, no one hesitated in dropping to the ground.

The power went out suddenly, and there was confusion and chaos. Cop lights pierced the darkness, and Haley and I ended up being corralled into the alley between two nearby houses to hide. Sharing the hiding spot with us were a couple of clowns, a life-sized puppet that looked like some demented Disney cartoon, and local circus hero Fred Normal, who stood on the tallest stilts I'd ever seen, pressed against the wall of the house, trying to be stealthy. Rumors began circulating about what had happened and it was agreed upon that someone had let go of a Mylar balloon, those shiny silver balloons that you get in hotel gift shops, that had somehow hit the power lines in a way that made the transformer blow.

A good thing to know if you ever need to knock the power out real fast.

5. These Are The People in your Neighborhood…
The house was across the street from RJ's, a bar frequented by the tiny

redneck population of the mostly black neighborhood. The bar's clientele was raucous, drunk and loud at all times of the day. One regular, Johnny Fishcakes, had a laugh like a pirate that was so loud it once woke my roommate up, from inside the bar, all the way across the street from our house. Another night I was woken up at three in the morning, about three hours before I had to go to work, by the "Pina Colada Song" being blasted on the jukebox while everyone inside sang along. This was all pretty annoying, but it kind of gave us some insurance that they would probably never call the cops on us for anything: Not for having fires in our backyard, or for setting off fireworks in the street — not for having punk bands play in our living room or for me living in my van on the street. In fact, the van gave us even a little more leverage, because, with its high-top roof, it gave the redneck dudes from RJ's the perfect cover to smoke weed.

It was a loud block. There was a band that practiced white boy country-blues across the street, and Billy, who played in a Janis Joplin tribute band, drunkenly practicing the piano next door to us and Charmaine, the insane drunk that would sit across from RJ's screaming obscenities at everyone inside the place. (I always thought Charmaine was homeless until one day I rode by what was apparently her apartment, where she sat in the living room, with the door open, screaming at her TV.) Despite all of this, though, life on the block went pretty smoothly for quite some time.

There were minor altercations, for sure: Once, my life was threatened by a RJ's patron who I'd never seen before. He was the kind of guy commonly referred to colloquially as a "Yat," a loud-talking white suburbanite with the smacking Irish-descended accent found only in Louisiana and around New Jersey. The guy was blind drunk at one o'clock in the afternoon. I was helping an acquaintance jump her car and the guy was mad that my van was in the middle of the street, blocking his truck. His complaint would've been reasonable enough, except for the fact that I wasn't actually blocking his truck, and he had about eight feet of clearance on the driver's side of my van (which was pretty amazing since the truck, a gleaming new F-9000,000 or something, was huge, the size of a dwarf planet at least). I pointed this out to him and he responded by grabbing me by the neck and telling me, in slurred words that he spat at me, "Maybe Ah'll jutht go get my fuckin' gun and thoot your ath." He went back to his truck and began rooting around for the gun. I went over to RJ's and threw open the door. Normally it was locked and you had to be buzzed in after the bartender checked you out on the camera (which, as rumor had it, was a way to keep Black people out of the bar) but today it was open.

"Can y'all come get your drunk asshole?" I called into the boozy cave. "He's going to shoot me!"

The bartender, a woman from New Zealand who I'd spoken to quite a bit, came out and surmised the scene. Drunk Yat guy had been unable to find the gun and had kind of fallen asleep leaning half in and half out of his pickup.

"Why don't you move your van, then?" asked the bartender. I hadn't wanted to move the van, mostly because it didn't have reverse and getting it right where you wanted it, especially in this case, where I had to be right next to the car I was jumping, was a skilled chore. Also all of the streets in New Orleans are tiny, since they were built a long time ago for carts and the like, not for huge vans and stupid redneck trucks. Consequently most of them are one-way streets, meaning that, for me to drive around the block, I actually had to drive around, like, *five* blocks, and the little orange gas pump on the dash was already lit up. But the maniacal redneck had come to and gone back to his search for the gun, and the New Zealander bartender had made it clear where her loyalty stood: toward the dude who tipped her. Though it seemed to me that by helping this guy get into his car, she was probably sending him (and potentially a bunch of innocent bystanders) swerving off to a fiery death. The lady I was giving the jump to had locked herself in her car and was just watching all of this unfold. I looked at my options and decided not to get shot.

"Fine," I said, unhooking the jumper cables. The truck, the redneck and the bartender were gone by the time I had burned a gallon or so of gas in my gigantic, falling-apart van, just to get back to where I'd started.

"You know when we leave here," my roommate Colin prophesized later, "it'll be because of a war with RJ's."

Actually, though, we just ended up hating each other and moved out.

6. The Weather Up There

I got a job stilt walking.

It worked more or less like this: Really boring people from out of town, say, software programmers or telephone company consultants, would decide that, for their next conference, they wanted to do something reeeeaaaallly fun. Upon slight introspective soul-searching, though, they realized that they had no idea how to do that or what it might be. Then they called Peter Pope.

Peter Pope was part of the vanguard of the New Orleans entertainment industry, ruling over our city with an army of stilt-walkers, jugglers, revelers and bigheads. Peter and rival Marcy Mars fought for control of the city's supply of fun. So for conferences, for grocery store openings, for corporate parades (which are like embarrassing scaled-down replicas of the normal parades, *sans* floats, where about thirty middle-management types walk around the French quarter going "Whooo!" and throwing beads at each other), Peter puts together a package of entertainment that's just right for the event. Maybe the hotel ballroom where your event is booked needs a fortune teller. Or how about a contortionist? Need a dwarf? No problem. And if a stilt-walker is called for, Peter would call me. (Well, actually he'd call a couple of more professional stilters with better hygiene, and if they weren't available, or thought they were above tromping around at the Albertson's grand opening, then he would call me. I was like the embarrassing little brother of the New Orleans circus-arts community.) I'd head over to his office, a mauve house on Marigny Street that was chronically decorated for Mardi Gras. There I would be given my outfit for the day: Uncle Sam, maybe, or George Washington, or a football player, or, if I was lucky, the French clown outfit with the pointy nose and hat. I liked that one, because it lent itself so well to mime that it got me out of having to respond to the inane comments of the event-goers.

"How's the weather up there?" was the old-stand by, usually coming from some middle-aged Midwestern guy, half-drunk on the complimentary Budweiser, showing off his scathing wit for his lady-friend. Sad thing was, as lame a taunt as it was, I never came up with a clever retort to it. And I wasn't supposed to. The second directive of the stilt-walker, behind being a walking signpost to remind people that they're having fun, is to take this dimwitted abuse, thus making the party-goers feel like they are not just *fun*, but funny.

I remember once when Peter Pope had me dressed up as a cowboy. "A Mardi Gras cowboy," he explained, meaning that I would be passing out beads in shiny cowboy garb in the ballroom of the Hyatt Regency. What he didn't explain was that it was for a conference of Republican sheriffs' deputies from Dallas. I was instructed by the promoter of the event, as the buzz-cutted deputies began to pour in, to stand by the door handing out my arsenal of beads and greet each party-goer with what the promoter called "a big ol' *Howdy*!" Each deputy trickled in, indiscernible from the last, wife in tow, and every one considered himself quite the jokester: "How's the weather up there?" was in fierce competition with "Now that's what I call a long, tall Texan!" I lost track of which remark was ahead, though, when the promoter of the event came around to tell me that my "Howdy's" weren't up to snuff.

7. The Pigs

Taylor and I, the first time we ever hung out, decided to go for a drink. Taylor was the friend of a friend, and had been sleeping under the ping pong table at her house, right around the corner from mine. We'd met a couple of times, but didn't really talk until this night, when we ran into one another on Decatur Street in the Quarter. On our way to find a suitable bar, we biked through Bourbon Street. It was a Friday Night, and getting anywhere meant artfully guiding our big delivery baskets through the crowds of Polo-clad potential rapists that, each weekend, got vomited up by universities around the country and came oozing down to New Orleans. Navigating the throng was even trickier for me than usual since I was carrying in my basket my tiny, nervous Chihuahua, Pixote.

At one point I heard someone yelling "Hey! Hey, stop!" at us. Glancing around at the crowd of novelty-drink-wielding zombies, I didn't really feel like stopping.

When Taylor, Pixote (pronounced Pee-sjoe), and I pulled up to The Emerald Aisle Bar, our point of terminus, Taylor said, "we just got yelled at by an officer of the law." And, being new in town, he wondered what proper etiquette was in such a situation. "Well," I said, "I'm not sure what Fodor's or Lonely Planet would say about it, but maybe we should hide." We made our way through the crowded front room of The Emerald Aisle, past the video poker junkies and off-work exotic dancers. In the tiny back bar, I told the bartender, a girl with a dyed black beehive haircut held together by chopsticks, "We just got chased by the cops, can we hide out in here?"

"Sure thing," she said, but upon spinning around to face us from where she'd been pouring someone's shots, she got a dour look on her face and added, "Oh…but you'll have to leave the dog outside. We just started serving food."

I carried Pixote out to the sidewalk and tethered him to the lamppost, grumbling about living in a town where the Health Inspector has more clout than the Fuzz.

8. Urine Trouble

Public urination in the French Quarter during Mardi Gras is a big game of cat and mouse. The city does everything in their power to make you pee in the street, short of speakers that blast the sound of running water, I guess. There aren't any bathrooms, you're sipping on an oversized novelty drink (which you couldn't have possibly resisted due to the overwhelming charm of the guy in the inflatable Hand Grenade outfit at the bar where you got the drink) and the whole place reeks like pee anyway. What do you do? You slip behind a car, or a horse and buggy, or a pile of novelty drink cups, and let go, hoping that the cops don't catch you. If they catch you, they drag you down to Orleans Parish Prison and throw you into the waiting room with all of the other drunks and public-urinators. In all likelihood, you are some well-off college kid or businessman who just wants to get this over with, get back to Iowa and pretend this never happened (because, in lots of cases, those relying on you to be there probably didn't realize it *was* happening, or that you were even in New Orleans at all). So you just pop your little card into one of the thirteen or so ATMs that are conveniently located in the holding tank, pay your bond, and go on your drunken, free-peein' way. If you don't have the little plastic card, or the funds to pay your way out, then you get thrown into general population with all of the lowlifes that got busted during the pre-Mardi Gras sweeps: mostly known crack-heads that are easy busts for the cops, New Age dudes arrested for reading tarot cards without a permit, or drunks. Of course, if you're lucky, since OPP doesn't separate misdemeanors from felonies, you might get to make some interesting new pals.

One Mardi Gras, Ski got caught peeing in the Quarter. The cops, feeling generous, offered him an alternative to OPP.

"If you wipe it up with your coat," they told him, "we'll let you go." Ski opted for jail. Across the Quarter at about the same time, Joel got caught for the same offense, and was offered the same option by different cops (which is scary because it means they sit around talking about this shit), and was so drunk that he removed his coat and used it to mop up the puddle on the sidewalk. The cops made him put it on and took him to jail that way.

9. Jollies
One morning I woke up and decided to go to the bar, which had begun to have brunch on the weekends. I stumbled out into the oppressive sun and made my way, barefoot, down the crumbling Ninth Ward sidewalk. When I got to Vaughan's, the corner bar that had ping pong tables and where local jazz legend Kermit Ruffins played each week, something caught my eye. There was a cardboard box lying on its side on the ground, in a spot where the sidewalk turned from grass to sunken, crumbling brick. Out of the box had spilled a pile of crawfish, some dead, some crawling instinctually toward the river with their last strength. They were dark, almost black, and on each one's back was a number, written in white-out. Oh Jesus, I thought, they were racing them! I could totally picture a gaggle of redneck guys gathered around the ping-pong table, hooting encouragement and placing bets on the panicked crustaceans. When the brutal clarity of sun-up set in, maybe they wondered why it had seemed like such a good idea before throwing them out on the sidewalk to die, or fend for themselves, which is how I found them.

10. Notebooks in Atlantis
What do I say to explain how it was?

Mr. P was ninety years old. He always looked good, dressed to the nines in a v-neck sweater and cap. All he ever said was, "Hey, hey, alright, alright." And he got treated like the fucking mayor.

Do I tell you that? Does it help explain how amazing where we lived was?

Or do I tell you how bad it could be. How that one summer everyone got robbed, and, for some reason, they all had their cameras stolen? Or that Haley and I were the only people I knew that never got mugged?

Do I tell you about the pauper's cemetery, where people who couldn't afford expensive above-ground tombs would bury their dead marked with whatever they had, with bike wheels spray-painted gold and old chairs and beer bottles? And sometimes the bodies would resurface, bones and skulls popping up out of the crumbly, moist earth.

What do you want to know?

About Nutria rats?

About Ernie K. Doe and his Mother-in-Law Lounge? And how supposedly, Ernie K. Doe, the aged rhythm n' blues star, had a transmitter in the Mother-in-Law that sent out a looped recording of his voice saying "I AM THE EMPEROR OF THE UNIVERSE....I AM THE EMPEROR OF THE UNIVERSE..." over and over again to the confusion of any AM radio listeners who happened to be driving by.

Tell me what you want to hear, jog my memory, because, amongst all the dancing, the partying, I didn't stop to write it down. Deep down, we all knew we were dancing and partying in a sinking city, but when that city makes you feel more alive than ever before; when every color and bleat of a trumpet seems clearer and crisper than it possibly could anywhere else, it's easy to forget about the danger all around you.

11. New Levels

Some nights, while I was living in my van in front of his house, Desmond and I would leave our neighborhood and bike into the Quarter just to sit on this one particular stoop. In New Orleans you can drink on the street, so some nights, when the weather is nice and there's no one out, it seems ridiculous to go to a bar. The stoop we'd picked out was pretty nice, right across from Bastille Mart, so we could get our dripping po' boys and beer and just settle in for a while. The only problem was that if you let your head hit the shutters on the door behind you, the lady that lived there would get mad. You can only drink so many tall cans before you forget and let your head fall back and next thing you knew the cops would be there.

Funny things would happen on that stoop. That's where we met John, a drunken carpenter who sang us a song about burying pigs. Apparently we appreciated the pig song more than the woman in the house, and soon the cops were there. They ran all of our names and it came up that John had been arrested for public drunkenness thirteen times.

Once I had eggs thrown at me on that stoop, another time a bottle, both hurled from passing cars that I couldn't catch up to, though I tried.

The strangest thing that we ever saw on the stoop happened one night when the power had gone out in our neighborhood. A thick fog had dropped onto the city, and we'd just bought some sandwiches and some beers and were getting comfy on the stoop. Along comes this guy so drunk he can't stay on the sidewalk. He's reeling from one side of the street to the other. He lurched past us, barely avoiding an open water meter hole. (The City of New Orleans, which cannot afford to repair its crumbling streets did, at some point in history, foot the bill to have cast a bunch of ornate water meter covers. They have this crazy crescent moon and stars design that inspires people to steal them, so that there are a lot of open meter holes in the sidewalks. Obviously, when you combine holes in the sidewalks with drunk people, hilarious antics oft ensue.) Then, as though coming out of his blackout, the guy stopped, suddenly gripped by a sense of great purpose. He headed over to a pole supporting one of the hundreds of huge wrought-iron balconies in the Quarter. He shimmied right up it like it was nothing and climbed over onto the balcony. "Holy Shit!" barked Desmond and I in unison, inbetween bites of po' boy. "That guy must've done great in gym class," Desmond said. We watched in awe as he climbed over the rail of the balcony and pressed his face against the glass doors of the apartment it was attached to. Apparently liking what he saw, he tried the door. Locked. The second one, however, was not. He went in.

"Maybe he lives there," I said.

He didn't.

It took about three seconds for the screaming to start, and a second after that the guy came stumbling backwards through the doors and back out onto the balcony, followed by some extremely angry young men who did, actually, live there. Without any hesitation, the trespasser stepped back over the wrought iron railing and made the twelve-or-so-foot fall to the sidewalk. He rolled as he hit, righted himself, sprung up and pounded on the hood of a parked Mercedes, just for good measure. This set off the car alarm, which frightened him, and he took off running down the street toward Jackson Square.

Ten minutes later the cops showed up in full force, three cars of them, to inspect the scene of the crime. They walked around, checking out the balcony from all angles, calculating the trajectory of the guy's fall, quizzing the people who lived in the apartment about any possible motive for the break-in.

"Should we tell them that it was just some wasted guy?" I asked Desmond.

"Naw, I don't think so," he said, finishing his po' boy and tossing the greasy paper wrapping into the nearby garbage can.

12. More Cops

A guy named Cassady got hit by a car. He'd been riding his bike the wrong way down a one-way street, and the people in the minivan who hit him told him it was his fault. He left his front teeth laying in an intersection. When he called the cops, they told him that a cyclist in New Orleans was expected to get off of the bike at each intersection, walk through, then get back on the bike. They left without taking a report from him.

Another cop stopped me one day on my way to work to tell me that I was supposed to be riding on the sidewalk. As she said it, I pointed to the pile of gravel that passed for the sidewalk in our neighborhood; it was really just grass now, the broken remains of the concrete barely even visible from where we stood.

"You mean *that*?" I said.

"That's the law," she said.

"No it isn't!" I argued, and when she asked if I wanted to see the law for myself I said that I would. She pulled a white, three-ring binder out of her trunk. The smirk on the cop's face betrayed what a joke this whole rigmarole was; that we both knew that the law of New Orleans was a nebulous and meaningless thing. Rumors were spread amongst the lowlifes of the Quarter, excited tales repeated again and again over beers about this friend of that friend that was arrested for "leaning with intent to fall" or "assaulting a cheeseburger." I heard so many different versions of these stories from so many drunks and traveling punks that I stopped believing any of them. If someone started to tell a "leaning with the intent to fall" story, it was a signal for me to stop listening to anything they said. "Man, my buddy Spacebag was just leaning on this wall," some guy with face tattoos and a dog might say, or "I was spanging on Decatur and some fucking yuppie gave me a cheeseburger, and I didn't want a cheeseburger. I wanted a forty so I threw it on the ground, and then the cops came up and…" As soon as these stories started, I started looking for an escape route.

And whether or not anyone was ever arrested for those particular offenses doesn't matter much, because the cops have made it clear again and again that they can nab you for pretty much any offense they want.

The cop failed to find the law about riding on the sidewalk (it isn't there, though it is illegal to ride with no hands), and after threatening to arrest me for my attitude, ultimately let me go to work.

After that I got frustrated. In a society with so many laws, I thought, how come no one knows what any of them are? When I was out delivering food one night, I decided to go straight to the source. As I rode past the French Quarter police station on Royal and Conti, I stopped. I locked my old Schwinn Collegiate up next to the huge fiberglass sculpture of a uniformed fish devouring a black-and-white-stripe-clad prisoner, and went inside.

At the desk was a cop with a face like a ferret's. Suddenly I remembered him from my one time being arrested in New Orleans. After I'd gotten out I'd spent a week going to the station every night trying to get back a pocketknife that they'd taken from me when they took me to OPP. Over and over again I went there to get my knife, and over and over again the ferrety cop had given me the run-a-round. "I don't know," he'd say. "There's no record of a pocket knife. In fact, there's no record of your arrest."

"Well," I told him several times. "I definitely went to jail."

"Are you sure?" he asked.

"What? Yes I'm sure!"

"Well you're going to have to go to the station on Rampart and get a record of your arrest."

I went to the station on Rampart, where I was summarily ignored by two cops for at least twenty minutes, while they ate and talked on the phone, respectively. Man, I thought, I'm glad I don't have an emergency, because I would be totally screwed. Eventually one of the cops realized that I wasn't going to leave.

"You want something?" she asked.

"Yeah…I do." I explained the situation. She rolled her eyes and said she didn't know what she could do about it.

"What? Can't you look and see if there's a record of me getting arrested."

She rolled her eyes again.

"What?" I barked. "What is so difficultt here? I just want my damn knife back!"

She stared at me. The other officer, also a woman, was still on the phone, but stopped talking in mid-sentence. I knew that I had made a mistake. Not by getting angry, or even by raising my voice. In New Orleans, most everyone is angry and screaming their brains out most of the time. You can scream all you want. But I had *cussed*. New Orleans is any many ways, quite tolerant. This is a city where you can take over the streets with a mob of fire-blowing freaks and probably not get accosted. It's a city where, until a few years ago, you could drink in a car as long as you weren't the one driving (the "honey, hold my beer" law, someone called it). And even now, to protect the multitudes of drive-through daiquiri shops in the city (who are really the ones running things), you are allowed to drive with a drink in the car as long as it has a lid, a straw, and the tip of the little paper straw-sleeve that it came in is still on the straw.

But, man, if you cuss at someone, well that's just it. In disputes at both the French Quarter Post Office and at Louis Armstrong International Airport I made the mistake of saying the word "shit" under my breath. Both times the employees on the other side of the counter freaked out. It was like I'd said the Secret Word on Peewee's playhouse, and everyone just went ballistic. The cops got called each time.

That day at the police station, when I said the word "damn," they freaked out, but weren't quite sure what to do or who to call. "Oh no," said the woman that had been on the phone. "Don't you come up in here swearing."

"Uh-uh," agreed the other woman, the one closest to me. "Why are you going to come up here cussing at us?"

Then I lost it. I felt the same way I'd felt when I'd lay down on the side of the highway while hitch-hiking in Kansas, just to be passed again and again by motorists. I felt like I had just been told that I'm actually an alien, who was put on this planet by mistake, and the whole thing was just a mix-up from the beginning. Maybe I hoped that was the case, and that I would now get to return to my rightful home-planet.

But even so I still wanted my pocket-knife.

"Look!" I said. "I went to jail! I got out! I just want my stuff back!"
"Why are you yelling at us?"

"What do you mean 'why?' BECAUSE I FUCKING HATE COPS!"

Now, as you can imagine, this is a bad thing to scream in a cop station. Like teasing a gorilla's baby, expressing hatred for cops is something that is just generally not done. And if it is, it's done anonomously in zines or spraypainted in alleys, not at the top of your lungs in their clubhouse.

The woman at the desk just pointed at the door.

"Go," she said.

"But — I want my stuff," I said.

"No. Just go."

"Or what? Are you going to arrest me again?"

"Yes."

Back at the other station, in front of the weasely guy: "Yeah, uh, they couldn't find any record of the arrest, either."

And then we started over where we'd started, with him making excuses. Luckily this time, there was an off-duty lieutenant a few feet away. Overhearing our conversation, he came over and asked what was going on. I explained.

The lieutenant had turned to the desk cop and said, "Officer, will you *please* get on the phone and get this man his property?" which the guy proceeded to do.

So, the next time I was there, when I went to find out about the cycling laws, when I found myself once again in front of that less-than-helpful desk cop, I really hoped that he wouldn't remember me. If he did he didn't let on.

"Can I help you?" he asked, looking down at me from a cartoonishly tall desk.

"Yeah, I had a couple of questions about the law."

"Okay," he said. "Shoot."

"Someone told me that if you are cycling in the city, you have to ride on the sidewalk. Is that true?"

"No," he said, as though he were holding back from adding the word "*dumb-ass!*" "That's not true."

"Another uh, *person*, told me that if you were cycling and came to an intersection that you had to then get off of the bike, walk it through the intersection, and get back on. Is *that* true?"

The guy looked around, possibly hoping that someone was witnessing this. "How," he said, "in your mind, could you even entertain the idea of that being true?"

"Well," I told him, "it was a couple of your co-workers that told me that."

"Oh for the love of Christ," he said, then told me the completely unsurprising cycling laws of the city of New Orleans.

"Thanks," I said as I left. "Just checking."

13. So, What Do You Do?

I got a job at an architectural salvage place, a big warehouse that accepted donations of building supplies. I got paid six bucks an hour along with a motley crew of punks, drunks, college kids, one out-of-work actor (who hadn't been informed that he was no longer on stage) and a sixty-something-year-old woman named Velma. Our boss was Barbara, the suburbanite ex-manager of a dollar store who had somehow landed this position performing a community service for a neighborhood that she was afraid to walk through. Under her leadership we were getting paid six bucks an hour to root through the stuff people donated. Needless to say that in one of the poorest cities in the country, where everyone is struggling to maintain houses and buildings over a hundred years old, whose foundations sit on ground the consistency of tapioca, people didn't feel like donating very much. The place turned into a dumping ground for mismatched trim and congealed paint, weird modular storage units that no one remembered how to assemble, rusty nails and occasionally things that we couldn't even figure out what their use had ever been. Running the place was a bit like trying to maintain order in the boiler room at the tower of Babel. The days consisted of de-nailing trim, attempting to not get tetanus, running after wealthy slumlords who were shoplifting, literally watching paint dry, and putting up with the manic ramblings that streamed forth from the mouth of the out-of-work actor.

"Ooh look, someone donated a thousand little wooden sign posts," he said. "Maybe we can have a sale for vampire hunters." Or another time: "Oh look at all this hose. We could use this as snake storage." Or "Have you ever held a girl's hand while going down on her? They really like that."

Occasionally Barbara would wander through and ask what we were doing, tell us some long, pointless story about her days at the dollar store, then go back to solitaire or minesweeper or whatever it was she'd been doing on her computer. Eventually, I tired of my duties and instead spent my time out in the lumberyard next to the place, either napping in one of the dozens of claw-foot tubs that were out there or shooting at bottles with a slingshot. I'd go poke some cans of paint with a stick to see if they were dry yet, or smash old screen doors, which I liked doing pretty well. One day I was working with this kid Neil, a college kid who tolerated the job by aid of a serious intake of homegrown marijuana. We were demolishing a tool shed that had been rotting in the sun and rain of the lumberyard for a couple of years. I went to rip a hunk of siding off of the thing with a crowbar and in doing so, catapulted a colony of ants onto Neil and myself.

"Whoah," said Neil, his reaction time slightly dulled.

Duller than mine at least, because I was already out of the lumberyard and around the other side of the fence, yelling "Fuck this!" as I threw my work gloves on the ground and swatted ants off of myself simultaneously.

"Where are you going?" Neil said.

"I'm going back to college!" I yelled. When I got home, I felt better. I didn't go back to college, but I did stop showing up for work.

That was only one of an endless seeming list of terrible jobs I held in that city. I worked for two days as a dishwasher at an Italian restaurant where I had to work from midnight until nine a.m. My only company during the shift was a wide-eyed waiter who would stand at the mouth of the dish-pit and compulsively flip a butterfly knife while giving me a play-by-play account of what it was like his last time in the mental institution. At a pizza place on the edge of the Quarter I worked bike delivery (a New Orleans institution, and the most-coveted job in the French Quarter) at a place where, in my brief stint, two employees were almost stabbed by another employee, a guy named John. It took me a while to figure out what it was John did there besides occasionally show up and scream crazy nonsense.

Once I heard John yelling into the receiver of the phone: "Yeah Bitch, don't tell me how it is, I'm telling you how it mother-fucking is and if you don't fucking like it, I'll come on over there and show you how it mother-fucking is, YOU FEEL ME?" This last part was his trademark; he said it after everything like some sort of nervous tick, and when he did, his voice would get really high, coming to a crescendo on the drawn out FEEEEEEL, which he emphasized by standing on his tip-toes as he did it. After he'd hung up the phone, I checked the caller ID to see just who it was that was going to be shown how it mother-fucking is. It was the owner of the restaurant, our employer. Eventually I learned that John was the one who baked the bread, which, according to the menu, was "world-famous." He was, apparently, the only person who knew how to do this, hence his job-security. When he went to jail after the second attempted stabbing, the manager of the place, a chubby guy who had worked there forever and oozed hatred, sat at the bar looking worried. Occasionally he would slam a fist on the top of the bar and yell, "Dammit! If only we knew how to bake that bread!"

Around then I decided to sever my ties with that place, as I had all the others. So in the middle of my shift I hopped on my bike and rode around until I found a different Neil, a friend who'd just gotten to town. Neil was hard-up for work, and so when offered a job he jumped at the chance. We rode back over to the restaurant together. Inside, my co-workers, probably too busy fretting about John the homicidal baker, hadn't noticed my absence.

"Hey y'all," I said to the handful of workers in the kitchen. "This is Neil. He'll be your new delivery guy." They mumbled something resembling agreement, and I went home.

14. More Chaos

All of these details — the jobs, the run-ins with cops and arrests, shitty weather — were just the hum-drum, day-to-day things that filled the time in New Orleans, along with visits to the Food Stamp office, mediocre po' boy sandwiches, flat tires caused by the broken glass and pothole filled streets. And then came the holidays, and suddenly the city would fill with the people you'd forgotten about, who it turned out had moved away years before, and suddenly we'd all be out in make-up, dancing in the streets to a marching band, drunk again and wondering why our anarchic city couldn't just always be that way.

I remember one Lundi Gras when the ragtag group of clowns and puppeteers known as the End of the World Cirkus hosted the first annual Bumper Cart Ball. The Ball was a kind of demolition derby in an alley where teams had prepared to do battle with shopping carts with cut up tires, armor and decorations. Each team was two people strong: one pushing and one riding. The event was in a wide, open alley between two Ninth Ward warehouses.

By the time I got there the party was going strong: DJ Karo had his turntables set up atop a burnt-out Jeep that had been in the alley for months and a hundred or so costumed mutants were either being pushed around in, pushing around, falling out of, or cheering for the shopping carts. Electronic music thumped along with the madness. Fireworks went off randomly, and Ed the Clown, the driving force behind this theater of the deranged, was running around in a plaid suit and giant *papier-maché* shoes, screaming through a traffic cone. The cops arrived shortly, which, believe it or not, was most unexpected. It was actually only one cop. One cop against an army of lunatics who didn't seem to be from around those parts, who seemed to have actually just been shuttled back from the apocalypse to party here, on this nervous, lonely, rookie's beat. His eyes shot from side to side, trying to figure out who could possibly be in charge of it all. Could it be the guy in camo pants hurriedly packing away his turntables atop the blackened Jeep? Or the checker-suited clown with the traffic cone? How about the dreadlocked guy with shoulder pads made of carpet and gold penises springing from the sides of his skull?

Before the cop could decide who to hone in on, he was distracted by a young man in a tight, pink tank top and cowboy hat who ran out of the crowd, and assumed the football center position in the front of the cop. In one graceful motion the kid flipped his kilt up and shoved a lit Roman candle into his own ass. The cop just stood there, trying not to show fear as the fuse burned down. The crowd, all trying to gather up their accoutrements and friends and flee the scene, stopped, mesmerized by what was taking place. Then a flaming ball shot out of the Roman candle and meandered drunkenly up out of the alley to a point high above the cop's car, which was still running. The ball was followed by another, and another, and it wasn't until the fourth that the cop, probably re-considering his choice of career, or calculating how long he had to save before moving away from this place, approached the young man, still bent over, and said, "Sir! You must put that out immediately!"

The offending party yelled something unintelligible, and the cop again ordered him to desist. He didn't, until all ten of the flaming balls had discharged from the firework. (This Roman candle, perhaps sensing its important role in history, was perhaps the first one of those things to actually work like it was supposed to.) At that point he removed the smoking tube of cardboard from his anus and stood up. His face was flushed from being upside down. At this point the crowd sprung back into action like a football game coming out of a freeze-frame, all of them trying to get away and blend into the hoards of revelers out in the streets.

"I told you to put that thing out!" said the cop to the human pyrotechnics display.

"Sorry man," said the kid. "I couldn't! Trust me. When you're in that situation, you just gotta let them burn out on their own."

15. Tomorrow I'll Mug You, Today It's Snowing

The non-drinking holidays don't stand out so much in my mind. I probably took those Easters and Thanksgivings and whatnot to wander the streets, enjoying the relative calm and looking at things in new ways. And of course, I remember the time it snowed on Christmas. There was a potluck at the anarchist bookstore, the Iron Rail Book Collective, and a bunch of punks and weirdos were hanging out in the big warehouse where the Iron Rail is housed, dancing around to Jamaican music in an attempt to trick ourselves into feeling warm.

All of a sudden someone looked out the window and said, "Holy shit, it's snowing."

We all ran out onto the empty street where, sure enough, it was snowing. Big white flakes as fat as cockroaches poured down from the gray sky. Dan and Mitchell ran around having a snowball fight. The next day even, there was still snow on the ground. I'd worked for a week at a pizza place in the quarter and when I showed up to work there was still a little snowman in the courtyard by the kitchen, with sticks for arms and sliced black olives as eyes. The pizza place was owned by a Turkish guy named Erhan who, for some reason, had hired me despite the fact that my very presence filled him with obvious, uncloaked contempt.

My co-workers would tell me about how Erhan would say things to them like, "Never mind Ethan. Ethan? He is a…piece of shit. Fuck him."

When he got to work that day though, Erhan was in a good mood and the first thing he said to me was, "Hey man, tell me, were you here for the snow?"

"Yeah, Erhan," I said. "I was here."

"I was not here, man. I was out of town. Tell me…the people, did it make them happy?"

I told him that yes, it had made people very happy, which it had. When I'd biked around my neighborhood Christmas night I'd seen people who would normally be screaming at each other in the street or ripping each other off on drugs hugging each other. When Erhan saw the snowman he laughed until his eyes watered and all day, during the many slow stretches in the kitchen, he would spontaneously start laughing and shaking his head and go look at the little snowman again.

16. Against Building Codes and the Laws of Physics
I moved into an apartment on France Street, near the Industrial Canal and the bridge that led to the lower Ninth Ward. The whole house felt as though it might fall apart at any moment. At night I'd lie in bed and feel the house jiggling from the trucks on Saint Claude Avenue, two blocks over. Once I dropped a bowling ball on my bedroom floor by accident. As I watched, the ball rolled quickly across the floor, stopped and mysteriously doubled back and rolled the other way.

Either my house just sank more, I thought, or it's haunted. It was a depressing place, but apparently not depressing enough for me since I promptly borrowed all of my neighbor's Joy Division records to listen to while I painted my bedroom maroon and black.

17. Time to Go
My stilt-walking work all dried up, and I burned my bridges at every half-decent delivery job in the Quarter by habitually not showing up on days like Mardi Gras or New Year's, when the whole town is drunk and craving pizza or something deep fried on stale French bread. I was reduced to combing the second-string delivery positions, the places that were in lame locations, or where the bosses were too cheap to pay their delivery boys decently or places that had just opened up and hadn't established their clientele yet. Soon I found myself working in the back of Minnie's at the Market. Minnie's is a New Orleans institution. The bar has a policy of not closing throughout hurricanes and the founder overlooks the affairs of the place from his regular spot, an urn bolted to the cash register. The bar is

wildly popular. The little hole-in-the-wall kitchen located between the main bar and the bathrooms, however, isn't such a prize. It is actually somewhat of a black hole of commerce and, since I've lived in New Orleans, has been probably five different restaurants. The incarnation it had taken on when I worked there was a place called Granata's, which was started by a high-strung little guy named Adam. The menu at Granata's was standard barfare, deep-fried items that come out of generic, frozen bags and, strangely, Twinkies. Deep-fried Twinkies. People actually ordered these things, usually (for whatever reason) strippers, and each time one got ordered the cook, an alcoholic of the shaky, muttering-under-his breath type named Stratton would complain about how goddamned hard it was to get a goddamned Twinkie to stay together in the deep fryer.

My job as delivery boy was, obviously, to transport the deep-fried Twinkies (and whatever else the strippers, t-shirt store guys, hotel and parking lot attendants and bartenders of the French Quarter might order). Unfortunately, though, they didn't order too much, and my job duties usually boiled down to sitting in the back bar beside the bathrooms, drinking beer and reading. Some nights my tab would be more than my tips.

The job was so slow, in fact, that I split my efforts between two bars. While home base was Minnie's, I also delivered for the The Emerald Aisle's new place, Black Cat; Black Cat was a kind of hipster-aimed diner/bar that was completely failing to get off of the ground. Occasionally someone might order something off of their overpriced menu, some tater-tots or something, and they'd call Minnie's to have me come over, pick it up, and deliver it. The bartender, Kelly, was a guy who had once shared the living room with me at a house where we were both staying. Thus he kind of took me under his wing in the best way a French Quarter bartender can: he gave me shots.

Some nights he would declare, "Tonight, we do a shot every time you HAVE a delivery." That night ended with me banging on the shutters of Black Cat because they had drunkenly closed up with one of my orders still inside.

I didn't make much money, but on warm nights, with whiskey in my belly, I didn't usually mind biking around, taking the fried Twinkies to the strippers, or portabella sandwiches to the house on Royal where they filmed hardcore gay porn. Occasionally, though, there were the bad nights, the nights where the drivers were just a little drunker than usual, or the tips a little shittier, or the customers a little snottier, and then every turn of the pedals seemed too hard and going to Bourbon Street one more time just sounded like a nightmare.

One night, as I left the bar with a couple of orders in my basket, I passed a couple of really wasted guys about a half block up Decatur from the bar. These guys were your typical drunken French Quarter guys. I don't know why these guys flock to New Orleans, because of Girls Gone Wild videos or what, but they sure are all over the place, screaming and fighting and sexually harassing women. In some way they provide a public service, by reminding those of us that lived there why we don't live anywhere else. At least in New Orleans they get quarantined to Bourbon Street and the surrounding blocks of the Quarter, thus being easy to avoid. Unless, of course, you are the lowly delivery-boy, forced to maneuver your big-basketed cruiser through the hordes of novelty-cup-wielding fuckwits.

On this particular night, I wasn't in the mood at all. Perhaps the hardcore porn guys had stiffed me or I'd been cut off by a car or been insulted and was a little too slow in coming up with the perfect come-back. I'm not sure what it was, but these guys made my jaw clench as soon as I laid eyes on them.

When one of them yelled, "Fuck this!" and threw his half full novelty cup on the street in front of me, I agreed.

Indeed, I thought. Fuck this.

I stopped my bike, picked up the plastic Tiki god or whatever the cup was shaped like, and rode to catch up with the guys. They were getting in their car, which was, predictably some huge American-made monster truck, the kind that they make extra loud so as to drown out the cries of Iraqi children.

I wheeled my Schwinn past them slowly and said, "Hey, you dropped this," as I lobbed the cup at their sweet ride. It felt like everything went into slow motion as the cup sailed through the air, catching the light of a streetlamp for a second before dropping into the bed of the truck. When the cup hit the bed with a soft "Thunk" though, everything snapped back into real time.

"OH YOU'RE DEAD, MOTHERFUCKER!" one of the guys yelled as he rounded the front of the truck and barreled after me. I stood up on the bike and pedaled as hard as I could. The guy's breath sounded like there was a freight train behind me and, as I rode, I kept thinking to myself: Now, I know that the bicycle allows me to go about five times as fast as the pedestrian, and there's really no way that this guy is going to catch me, but, goddamn, he must be a linebacker or something because he's getting really, really close to me!

What is the worst-case scenario at your job? Cooks, I imagine, probably ponder what to do in case of a shrimp shortage or an oil fire. The computer programmer worries about system failure and errors in code; the stilt-walker plans to fall. The bicycle delivery person plans on being assaulted by drunken rednecks. I had a plan for this, which was to turn immediately onto the first one-way street available and take it the wrong way, thus keeping them from following me in a car. The first cross-street I came to was Governor Nicholls, which, thankfully, was a one-way the wrong way. I turned onto it and heard my enraged pursuer's footsteps fall back. Thinking I was in the clear, I rode leisurely down Governor Nicholls, catching my breath. The place where I was going was some fancy coffee shop on Rampart Street, a large four-lane road that borders the French Quarter to the north. I was a block and a half from Rampart when I heard the squeal of tires to my right. I looked over to see the truck making the corner, fast.

They are not going to chase me the wrong way down a one-way street, I thought.

I was mistaken. The truck took the turn onto Governor Nicholls without any hesitation. They were right behind me then; the roar of the V-8 was all-consuming, as though every metal band in the world were playing at the same time, and chasing me. I spotted a driveway on my left, or what passes for a driveway in the Quarter, which is just a little ramp to get cars over the sidewalk and into a garage. I quickly jerked my bike over and up onto the sidewalk.

There is *no fucking way* that they will chase me onto the sidewalk, I thought. I was, of course, mistaken once again. All that saved me from becoming little more than a red-baron-style stencil on the side of these guys' truck was a lamp post in the middle of the sidewalk about three feet from the walls of the houses that we were passing. I squeezed my bike through the little patch of sidewalk between house and post, and the truck was forced back onto the street. We were nearing Rampart, the wide avenue on the lakeside of the Quarter, and as I attempted to steady the deliveries in my basket and keep them from spilling (because, although I was in imminent danger of being crushed beneath this F-9000 or whatever it was, I was still, above all else, a professional delivery boy), I realized that in mere seconds I would be coming off of a one-way street the wrong way onto a busy four lane road. The cars, now no doubt driven by slightly drunken tourists, would have no warning that a frightened cyclist was about to fly out in front of them.

Oh well, I thought, here I go.

I closed my eyes and held my breath as I shot out into the middle of Rampart Street. Images ran through my head of me splattered across the windshield of some SUV alongside the fried mushrooms and burgers in my basket. When I opened my eyes, though, Rampart Street was empty. No buses, no drunken tourists, no low-riders with Earth-shaking stereos. Just me and, a moment later, the testosterone-fueled monster truck that could. Apparently they weren't so into the idea of driving against traffic on a major road, so they got over into the lanes opposite me and floored it. When they came to a break in the common ground (the New Orleans name for the median), they pulled over into my lanes, blocking my path.

The guys jumped out and got into the gaps between the curb and their truck, taking stances like baseball catchers. I weighed my options. Because of the curbs there was barely anywhere for me to go, and if I turned around I would be back in the dark labyrinth of the Quarter, with nothing to stop them from chasing me around even more. The place I was supposed to deliver the (now slightly shaken) food was ahead of me another block. I decided to go for it. As I came up on their ad-hoc road block, the guy who'd been driving, a fuming, pink pit-bull of a man, barked orders at the other one in a thick southern accent.

"All right now, spread out, don't let him through."

I glanced over at the minion on the ass-end of the truck. He obviously wasn't as excited about this situation as the driver, and was perhaps even questioning what type of company he keeps. I stopped the bike and they held their ground, kind of dancing from foot to foot like they were trying to catch an escaped animal, waiting for it to dart. I swung the front end of my Schwinn around toward the more doubtful of the pair and took off straight for him. When the alpha-male guy took up chase behind me, I swooped around in a big loop and squeezed past the truck. I left the guys swearing, alpha blaming his stooge for my escape.

When I got to the café where I was supposed to be delivering the food, I leapt off of my bike with the bags in my hand. There was a woman, presumably the owner of the place, standing on the sidewalk in a sequined nightgown and loads of make-up, smoking a long skinny cigarette.

"These guys are trying to fucking kill me!" I blurted.

The woman didn't respond at all and just calmly continued to smoke her cigarette.

I said it again: "These guys are trying to kill me with their fucking truck, will you please call the cops?"

She flicked the cigarette onto the sidewalk and crushed it beneath a patent leather high heel and, with a hostility almost as thick as the pancake goop on her face, let out a sharp, "No."

No.

I felt like the fabric of reality was ripping around me. I had never even seen this woman before! Here I am, showing up in a total panic, telling her that some psycho is trying to run me over, and she won't help? Was she in on this? For the last couple of years I'd had the sneaking suspicion that the city of New Orleans was trying to kill me. I'd never brought it up with anyone because talking about that kind of thing gets you lumped into the type of social circles that sit in coffee shops talking loudly about their theories on Freemasons to whoever will listen. But it was true! The city was trying to kill me and it all had something to do with this Cruella DeVille look-alike who owned a café that I'd never even noticed before!

I ran past her, still clutching the paper bags of food in either hand. Inside the place a woman was baking cookies in a little kitchenette in the back of the room. It was warm and smelled good in there.

"Call the fucking cops!" I yelled. She dropped her baking sheet and started dialing. I explained the situation as she dialed.

Now (as I've made clear) I do not like the police. In fact, in New Orleans, the cops have never helped me. Instead they usually end up just being suspicious of *me*. (And not just when I'm yelling at them at the station.) In a few moments of sheer terror, however, I have forgotten my past experiences and turned to them for help, which I never get. This time was no different. The guys in the truck had looped around and driven slowly past the café, giving me the dagger eyes as they did. The cops, in typical style, showed up about ten seconds later. They looked frighteningly similar to my attackers, and I thought that maybe they would just get out and pummel me. They did not, but they didn't offer much help either. They just took a report and left, eyeing me, as always, with suspicion.

And I still had a delivery to take to a dark part of the Marigny neighborhood, over a mile away. I stayed on the sidewalk and small roads, cringing every time headlights rounded the corner. I made it to the house, which belonged to a regular customer.

"Hey man," I told the guy, "sorry if this is shaken up at all, someone tried to kill me with their truck on my way here."

"Uh…" he said, obviously not expecting this situation. "Are you ok?"

"Yeah, I'm ok. I'm just worried about the ride back to the bar."

"Shit, be careful," he said, then gave me a mediocre tip.

There was some sort of turmoil outside of the bar when I pulled up. A bartender who I barely knew — a loud, dramatic girl from the suburbs — was waving her cell-phone and screaming while a gaggle of our co-workers attempted to calm her. Among them was Adam, my boss who was holding an armful of deliveries that had piled up while I was gone. We could go hours without the phone ringing but as soon as I was busy, fighting to remain amongst the living, everyone in town got a hankering for fried Twinkies.

"Ethan!" the frantic bartender screamed at me when I piloted the bike up onto the sidewalk, "did you hit my truck with a bottle?"

I stared at her, speechless. Well, brain, I thought, we've had a good run, but apparently you've decided to take a hike. I've obviously gone completely insane. Maybe I *did* throw a bottle at this woman's car. Maybe nothing is what I think it is. Maybe caterpillars are going to begin crawling from my eyes.

"Ethan," said Adam, sweating, still cradling the brown paper bags in his arms and attempting to blow his foppish bangs out of his eyes. "Will you please take these orders?"

"Jesus Christ, Adam! Hold on!" I snapped. "What in the shit-hell is going on?"

"Well," said the bartender, "did you?"

"Look," I said as calmly as possible, "I think someone's been trying to kill me with your truck."

"Ethan!" said Adam. "We'll get this straightened out when you get back. Please take these orders."

"Okay, fine!" I scooped the bags into my basket.

I took off down Decatur Street the same way that I had gone when all of this had started. I was riding past Fiorella's, a seafood place that also offered delivery. As I passed, a waiter there that I knew yelled, "You nearly got our delivery guy killed!" At this point I'd given up on ever making sense of anything again, so I just kept riding. It wasn't until I got back to the block that it all started to come together. The delivery guy for Fiorella's was a guy named Ted, who pulled up beside me. We both pedaled our cruisers slowly, meandering past the boutiques and bars of lower Decatur Street so that we could talk.

"Man, what the fuck is going on?" he asked me.

"Dude," I said, "I was about to ask you the same question." We stopped before getting back within eyeshot of my place of work.

"All I know," said Ted, "is that I was leaving here with a delivery and before I even made the corner up there, I heard some motherfucker yell, 'There he goes!' and all of the sudden I've got some huge redneck dude grabbing me by the neck! He was about to break my damn nose when his buddy got up there and was all like, 'No that's not him, that's not him.'"

I looked Ted over. We were both wearing black pants and garage jackets, both had short brown hair and stubble, both wore black, plastic-rimmed glasses. "Shit Ted, I'm so sorry. Those dudes threw a cup on the ground and I was all pissed off already and threw it in the back of their truck."

"Man, whew," said Ted, shaking his head as if to shake off the experience. "Let me ask you something…was that guy not unusually fucking fast?"

"Yeah," I nodded, "he was very, very fast."

Minnie's was still in turmoil when I got back. The bartender had apparently not stopped screaming since I'd left. Adam was trying to calm her down, as was Joe, the back bartender.

"You!" the girl yelled. "You fucked up my truck." I thought she was going to hit me and I held up my hands, prepared to fend her off.

"Look, I don't know what's going on, but here's what happened." I told them the whole story, start to finish, as I knew it. When I was finished, the bartender girl, who'd turned a sickening shade of Lisa Frank pink, let out a shrieking howl that is how I would imagine it would sound if you were to breed a University of Arkansas fan with a rhesus monkey. Then she stomped off back inside. Everyone followed her back into the bar except for Joe, the back bartender, who lit a cigarette and laughed. I slumped against the brick wall beneath the hanging sign that said, "Minnie's at the

Market, A Safe House."

"Joe," I said with desperation shaking my voice, "what the fuck is going on man?"

He kept laughing. "Dude," he said eventually, "those guys that were chasing you? One of them was her boyfriend."

"You're shitting me."

"Wait—that's just the beginning. He's also her cousin, and he used to be a fucking cop!"

"What? She's dating her cousin? This is too weird."

"It gets weirder: The truck they were driving was *her* truck, and the whole time they were chasing you they were on the phone with her. The guy said that you threw a bottle at the truck and put a big dent in it."

"It was a plastic fucking cup! I threw it in the truck bed!" I hollered. Joe shook his head and laughed again.

"That's some fucked up shit," he said.

Before I left work, I talked to the bartender whose truck it was. "Look," I said. "I'm not going to dwell on this. I'm not even going to bring it up again. I just want to make it very clear what happened: Your boyfriend tried to run me over with a two thousand pound piece of steel. And that is just not right."

She looked at me, her face still flushed and, through gritted teeth, said, "And it was *my* two thousand pound piece of steel." It made me feel slightly better that her anger had been re-directed toward her psychotic better half, but not much.

18. Blood

It was right before I left New Orleans, a couple of nights before we'd have our last night up Lee's ass. I made plans to meet Taylor at a coffee shop in Mid City, where I'd been camped out, avoiding people, working on my resume for when I got to my new home, Asheville, North Carolina.

"What do you want to do tonight?" said Taylor, joining me at the table. I put my resume into my bag. "I don't care. Not drink, though. I've been hittin' the sauce too hard." We decided to go for a bike ride through City Park. It was March, already warm, and it was a good night to ride beneath the mossy oaks. We passed the Art Museum in the middle of the park and made our way around it. Some fancy ball was happening and after we'd gotten a ways up the road, Taylor stopped.

"Did you see that?" he asked.

"See what?"

"There was an open catering truck back there full of booze," he said.

"Oh goddammit," I said.

We looped back around and sat on a park bench for a while, scoping it out. Sure enough it was open. Sure enough it was full of booze.

"OK," I said. "Meet me out at the main road in ten minutes."

He took off, and I rode over to where the truck was parked. Leaning my bike against it, I hopped in and started rooting through the bottles. The caterers would no doubt be out any minute and every bottle I found had one of those pour spouts on it, which I didn't want in my bag. Eventually I found two bottles of nice Scotch. I shoved them into my courier bag and took off, riding my bike away into the darkness of the City Park oaks. I was almost to the exit where I was to meet Taylor when I felt something dripping down my back. I jumped off the bike and ran into the grass, slumping down in a shadow and dumping the contents of my bag out onto the grass: one broken bottle of Scotch, one full bottle, one journal, one slightly damp resume. I put the intact bottle back and continued riding, holding my journal and resume in my hand as I rode. When I came into a streetlight I discovered that I'd sliced my hand open on the broken Scotch bottle and was streaking blood across my resume. Oh Jesus, I thought, *you see? You see what living in this town does to you?* One minute you're minding your own business, trying to fucking *better yourself*, and the next thing you know you're biking around Mid-City covered in blood and scotch.

To make matters worse, Taylor wasn't at our agreed-upon meeting spot. The event in the museum was letting out and there were police cars all around the entrance to the park. I decided not to hang around and headed toward Taylor's house, only a few blocks away. As I rode past parked cop cars with the windows down, I realized that I reeked of booze. It felt as though a visible cloud of alcohol was trailing behind me as I rode past the cops who were lazily hanging out their windows, waiting to go home.

Don't mind me, I thought. Just riding home covered in blood and Scotch. I whistled to affect an air of innocence.

At Taylor's, his roommate answered the door. She was in her bathrobe, holding a book with one hand, her finger marking her spot. She stared at me from behind the security gate. "Hey Shanna," I said, "is Taylor here?"

"Um no…he's not. Are you OK, Ethan?"

"Look, I need to come in. I don't have time to explain. The cops haven't been here yet have they?"

Shanna made no motion to open the wrought iron door.

"Jesus, I'm just kidding Shanna. I'll explain in a second. Can I please use your bathroom?" A few minutes later I was all washed up. Taylor came back and the three of us drank the surviving bottle of Scotch. It was good Scotch.

19. Can I Please Just Get Out Of Here, Please?
My van was older than me, a huge, jaundice-yellow beast that I'd bought for four hundred dollars. It offended people when I drove the thing past them on the street. Every time I started the beast up, I felt like some government official was going to show up with certified papers ordering me to stop immediately.

And now I was going to drive it to Asheville, North Carolina, twelve hours from New Orleans, through the mountains. It was a terrible plan.

My friends asked me why I was going to Asheville. I didn't know. All I knew was that I'd been there twice, there was a couch where I was welcome, and I was going. I stuffed my belongings into the van, hugged and hugged Shelley and Dan good-bye in my driveway.

"Dude," said Dan. "I still think you should've painted that van like a big bumble bee."

"Yeah, probably," I told him. "I guess I was too busy worrying about keeping it running." There was one of those sort of final seeming pauses in conversation. I shrugged and said, "Well…see y'all. I'll call you with my new address…in Slidell." (Slidell is a suburb just across Lake Pontchartrain from New Orleans).

Forty-five minutes later the van threw a rod on the twinspan, the bridge across Lake Pontchartrain that leads into Slidell. I screamed and cursed and cried, desperate to go. A guy in a Toyota Camry pulled over. He was the ultimate New Orleans guy, a skinny, thick-voiced little Irishman in wraparound sunglasses with a Coors Lite tucked between his knees.

"Hey buddy, car trouble?" he asked.

"Uh…yeah," I replied, looking at the smoking van, thinking of all the vans I'd laid to waste in my life.

"You want a beer?" he asked and I wanted to scream. I wanted to tell him no, that all I wanted was to get off the Twinspan, out of New Orleans, away from people who offer you beers while operating motor vehicles at noon. He gave me a ride into Slidell. I had the great yellow beast towed back into New Orleans, where I scraped all the VIN numbers off, removed the plates and destroyed the title.

The next day I loaded all my belongings into a borrowed truck and was gone.

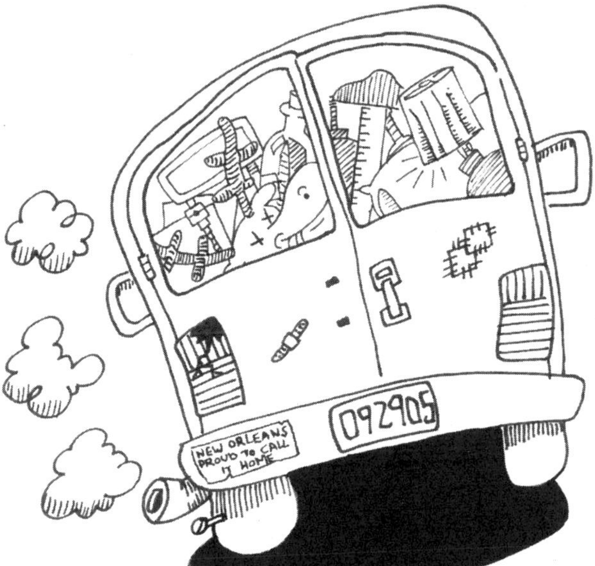

092905
NEW ORLEANS PROUD TO CALL IT HOME

NEWNESS

C AND I WERE SITTING on the porch, discussing our plans for spring, discussing the house we're both moving into across town.

"I'm addicted to newness," she said, when asked about why she was moving out of her idyllic punk house, which was right across the street from my chaotic one.

"Newness?" I asked. "Or turmoil?"

"Newness," she said firmly.

I concurred. It was my second spring in Asheville, and I too, at that moment, felt addicted to newness, even though C and I were both probably wearing the same shirts, pants, socks and shoes as when we'd met each other a year ago.

* * *

T and I went for a walk.

"Hanging out," she'd called it, an innocent moniker for "the big talk" that we both knew was coming. We sat in a clearing in the woods.

"I've been with him for five years," she said, "and I wouldn't trade that for anything." Then she added, "Though I do miss having crushes, and the newness of first kisses."

Then we made out for, like, three hours.

* * *

D and I were cooking some potatoes while everyone else nursed their hangovers in the driveway, watching the dogs sniff compost and idly picking at the gravel with sticks, smoking cigarettes, talking about their plans. I was whining about the situation with T.

"I'd like to give you advice," D said with his polished kind of "big brother" voice, "but I'm in the same boat, buddy."

"What?" I said, gasping as my coffee went down a little funny. "With whom?"

D said nothing, but his eyes betrayed him, shooting across the screen of his thick glasses. They might as well have had a little dotted line headed straight out the kitchen door to where E was rolling one of Z's smokes and sitting next to her boyfriend, J.

"NO!" I said.

He lowered his head and voice, stirred the potatoes and said, "Yup. Falling in love."

* * *

"It's never been like this before," A told me one night at L's house. He was describing his newest romance, possibly the twentieth one he'd described to me in the year since I moved to Asheville.

"We just sit around all day playing with each other's hair and shit."

He was wasted, sitting on the couch. A crowd of our friends were a few feet away, smoking in the door, but our conversation was concealed beneath the blaring Otis Redding record. It was "Sitting on the Dock of the Bay," possibly the only over-played classic of that type that doesn't drive me crazy. I love "Sitting on the Dock of the Bay." It's the song that Otis thought would be the beginning of a new type of music. He was dead four days after recording it.

"She's got a boyfriend," A added.

I've never felt the effects of spring so strongly as I have here in the mountains. Perhaps location is the reason. In the bigger cities of the Deep South, spring is a foreboding shift punctuated by an increase in drive-by shootings and new strains of mosquito-borne viruses. Here, though, it's just like children's books and love songs, just like fifties movies. Everyone gets all bonkers at the sight of each other's bare arms. Gardens and relationships get tilled, lofty projects begin. Some of us decided to start a metal shop, a place to build art and weird bikes out of junk we found. In the warehouse we rented down by the river, we tore down a room to replace it with another room. Our cars break down and we don't care, as long as the bikes hold together. There's even a new show space. We tried to get one together last year but a wave of evictions and fire marshal raids left everyone inert on their barstools. Some new blood though, new faces in town, new energy, and voila! The space for bands to play, which everyone talked about for so long, finally became reality. All ages, anything goes, shake your butt, rock out, just don't drink or pee outside. No one could think of a name for it though so B just picked one, and started putting it on flyers: *El Nuevo*. I like it.

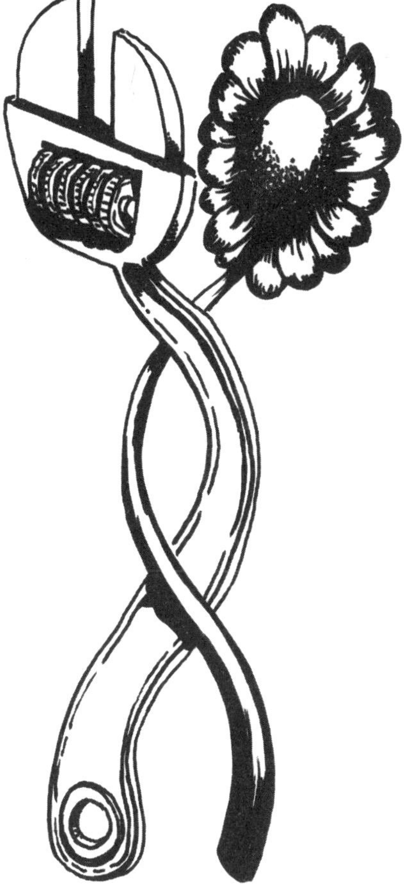

ASHEVILLE: MY ENABLER, MY HOME

WE WERE TELLING blackout stories again. Everyone was either hungover or getting drunk again, sitting around, playing Scrabble, and telling blackout stories. Sweet Tooth once came out of a blackout crossing the divider in the middle of the interstate. Robby once woke up after a blackout in the bed of a woman he'd never met, fully clothed and handcuffed to some guy named Chad, who'd pissed himself. Ted once came out of a blackout to realize he was in a strip club, and then threw up on himself. A friend of Blair's once came out of a blackout in a gas station parking lot. He had some guy he'd never seen before in a headlock and was punching him in the face. Once, at the hot dog stand where I used to work, my boss showed up blacked out, covered in vomit. "Chris," I asked him, "Is that your vomit?" He swayed around, trying to keep a bead on me and said, "Some of it."

Asheville is a drunk town. It's a lifestyle here, one that people defend more than anywhere else I've lived, and seeing as I moved here from New Orleans, that's saying a lot. According to AA, blacking out due to booze is considered a sign of alcoholism. In Asheville, it's offered as an excuse for all sorts of behavior, and one that doesn't require further explanation. Confront someone for breaking all your dishes, or eating all your food, or biting your friend repeatedly at a show, and you'll frequently get some mumbled response of, "Oh yeah, I don't want to talk about it…I was blacked out," as the offending party cracks open a tall can of malt liquor to start working on the next blackout. I once lived with a guy named Tony. We lived in a house called Bigside, a huge antebellum mansion that had been a total party house for a long time, the kind of house where you don't want to pass out with your shoes on (because that would mean that, in keeping with tradition, everyone still awake would have no choice but to write obscenities and draw penises all over you). Frequently, we'd find drunks we'd never seen before asleep on our porch, guided there in the middle of the night, apparently, by some boozy homing device. One night I was hanging out with Tony in his room. I got a phone call and left to take it. When I got off the phone I realized that Tony had gone to bed with my shoes in his room. I knocked on his door to get them. No response. I knocked again.

"Hey Tony?"

"Yeah! What?"

"Hey man, you got my shoes in there."

"Go away," he called back. "I'm blacked out!"

Whoah, I thought. Tony is so used to giving that excuse, he'd used it in the present tense! I'd never heard anyone do that before.

I won't claim never to have blacked out from alcohol. Once at a party in a small town in Missouri, I blacked out and spray-painted a skull and crossbones on someone's driveway. The girl, whose house it was, caught her landlord's wrath and had to clean it off, which she'd accomplished before I even rose from my cheap-beer-abetted slumber. She didn't seem too upset about it, and told me the story almost cheerfully.

"Shit, I'm really sorry…" I said. "Was it a good skull and crossbones at least?"

"No," she replied. "Not really."

I've blacked out arguments, before, and many a boring philosophical debate. I've even blacked out sex. These aren't things I'm proud of; I don't like not being in control. When I was younger, though, I admired the total maniacs, the weirdos who didn't care what anyone thought of them. Back then, the best way to earn my respect was to break into a fast-food place afterhours and steal all their hot dogs, or smash all of Tower Record's windows, perhaps. Now I realize that all those uninhibited wackos I held in such high regard weren't really the total bad-asses I made them out to be, they were just drunk.

These days, now that I've hopped on the booze train, I find myself acting that way, too. The bar closest to my house is right on the other side of all the government buildings (including the jail, the police station and the city building) from my house. I play records there on Thursdays, and they give me free drinks. I try to take it easy, but my shift is a long one, and sometimes I'm a little sloppy on the walk home through all those municipal buildings. There are days when I'll wake up, glad to be in my own bed, not exactly remembering taking my clothes off. I've climbed down out of my loft and looked around my room to find that I now own an emergency flare, a digital level and a manual of the city municipal codes. Oh yeah, that might come in handy some day, I guess. It always seems like a good idea at the time to go breaking into city trucks, storage sheds, or even the basement of the police station. Then, in the morning, as I make coffee, I remember the events of the night before and think how lucky I am not to end up mentioned in one of those weekly "dumb criminals" articles in the papers.

I don't always get away with my drunken antics, either. All riled up after a show in Memphis, I drunkenly decided it was a good idea to break into the zoo to look at the monkeys. I convinced my friend Ted that this was a good idea, too. When we got in we couldn't find the monkeys, and so looked at the snow leopards instead. Then we promptly got our asses arrested by some wise-cracking cops who kept telling us that, had we only waited twelve hours, it would've been the zoo's free admission day.

And I've injured myself, too. A drunken bike ride home one night, over a distance of about two blocks, ended with me waking up in the ER to an orderly pulling the now-empty case of beer out of my bag and making a "tsk tsk" noise at me. While my behavior concerned me, it didn't seem to bother my friends: When they came to visit me, in bed with a broken collarbone, they brought me beers to show their condolences.

After the bike incident, as well as some others, I decided to call it quits for a while. But Asheville doesn't like that decision; it doesn't know what to do with it. The whole city is like the friend who shows up with a plate of cookies the day you discover you're diabetic. One night, back at Bigside, where Tony and I lived with seven others, a group decision was made to take it easy with the booze. We ate a big meal, and after dinner, we spread blankets out on the floor so that we could watch a movie together. Tea and popcorn were being made when one of our roommates got a mysterious phone call. We only heard her end of the conversation: "What? Yeah, there's a bunch of people here. Nothing, just sitting here. Okay, uh…bye."

"Who was that?" we asked. She said she didn't know.

Five minutes later, just as the movie was starting, a small pack of our friends and acquaintances came stampeding into our living room, clapping and yelling, "Okay *move*!! Let's go, let's go! Get your shoes on, get your IDs! Let's go, people!"

We didn't question it. We jumped up and ran, flailing around the house gathering shoes, IDs and coats. We were then taken outside and herded onto the Party Bus, a kind of rolling dance-club-for-hire that just cruises around Asheville while the passengers on-board, well, you know… party. It had been rented out for the birthday of a girl I didn't even know at the time. They were making the rounds, abducting people from their homes while everyone on board drank beer and listened to a single Slayer album over and over again. I sat in the back of the bus with my roommates, looking dazed beneath the black lights. "Man," someone said, "you try to just have a relaxing night at home without booze, and, next thing you know, the mother-fucking Party Bus pulls up!" We let out a collective sigh and, admitting defeat, dipped into the cooler full of beer.

The most large-scale scene of Asheville's enabling tendencies came one September night. Some locals had been recruited to help work the Lexington venue Arts and Fun Festival, or LAFF. LAFF features artists' booths and food, some games and bike jousting, but is mostly just an excuse for tourists to walk around drinking huge beers in the middle of the street. As it got dark, the festival drew to a close and all of the tourists found their ways into bars or back to their bed and breakfasts or, unfortunately, to their cars. One of the organizers of the event asked some of my friends (who were milling around looking for funnel cake in the trash at the time), if they would help him pack some stuff up. "I'll give you a present," he said. They helped him load a bunch of tables and supplies into the back of a truck and the organizer-guy drove off. When he returned, he announced his "present." He told everyone they could help themselves to whatever was left of the beer, pointing to the big refrigerated truck full of micro-brewed keg beer. The next thing you know, a ragtag gang of punks and freaks were running around downtown Asheville, trying to find whatever containers they could to put the beer in: water bottles, random wine bottles, lidless quart buckets from restaurants, empty soda bottles, juice cartons, cups, a five-gallon carboy. Even as the truck pulled away, all the punks were running after it like baby pigs trying to get at their mother's teats.

The bounty was taken around the corner to a loft where some friends lived. By the time I got there, the place was wall-to-wall people. Every party-loving scenester in town was there, covering every inch of floor, chair, couch, table, counter, amp, fridge…and just pouring beer into themselves. I'd never seen anything like it. The party rambled on for hours, and I made a point not to drink too much of the seemingly endless supply of booze; I wanted to stay conscious enough to see (and remember) what ensued. There was a drunken gymnastics competition in the alley outside. Our party even staged a successful coup on a party next door. And of course there was tons of making out and near fights. Eventually, though, they all began to drop. The couches were covered with sleeping, beer-filled bodies. Our friend Ana slept outside in the back of someone else's truck, snuggling with a recycling bin. Eventually I conked out on a sewing table.

In the morning, I watched the other party-attendees slowly rouse themselves, shaking their cobwebby minds, trying to put the pieces back together. A guy named Andy slept face-down on one of the couches. "Man," he said. "I slept on something really fucking…*uncomfortable*." He reached beneath the cushions of the couch, found the offensive pea (a water-bottle full of beer, naturally) and dislodged it.

Patrick, who actually lived in the loft where all of this had transpired, came to and stumbled to the fridge. "Oh wow," he muttered. "Juice." He raised a carton of orange juice to his mouth to find that, of course, it was full of beer. "Oh, god! Shit." It was as if all the liquid in the world had turned to beer.

Seeing all of these die-hard Asheville drinkers grimacing at the sight or mere mention of beer, even really good beer, reminded me of that story about the monkey claw that grants wishes, all of which turn out to backfire on those making the wishes. But Asheville doesn't give up that easily. Eventually, everyone's tongues stopped feeling like sandpaper, their minds cleared, and they saddled back up to the bars. Asheville is a drunk town. Not only are people here off the wagon, but they're getting run over by all the other wagons in the caravan. And they don't mind.

SPARKS

I REMEMBER WHEN Sparks first came to New Orleans. I was reaching into the cooler at Donna's (the corner store on St. Claude Avenue where the beers always smelled so much like rotten meat you had to pour them into cups to make them drinkable) for a six-pack of Schlitz. There, in the little plastic "impulse buy" shelf attached to the inside of the cooler door, the one where bizarre trends in alcoholic beverages get shelved, was a bright, happy, orange-and-silver can declaring itself to be a "Malt energy drink," enriched with ginseng, guarana and something called "Flavor Unit."

Uh-oh, I thought. The crack dealers are not going to like this.

And while I was glad that these chipper little cans were there to brighten my nightly trips to Donna's and to distract me from the otherwise-gruesome scenery (the ice machine that was always dripping blood onto the floor, for instance), it wouldn't occur to me for several months to actually buy one, much less open it and put it in my mouth. It wasn't, in fact, until my random move to Asheville, North Carolina that I would finally experience the effects of Flavor Unit for myself.

I was helping set up a Valentine's Day party at Bigside, one of the big punk houses in Asheville (which I would later mover into). Some Bigside residents and I were sent to retrieve the Valentine keg from a local beer store, which happened to be having a close-out sale on Sparks. My friends asked why they were liquidating their Sparks inventory.

"Yeah, uh, we won't be carrying that stuff anymore," said the proprietor of the shop.

"Really? You don't sell kegs of this stuff?" asked one of the members of our posse.

"That'd be frightening," he replied.

That night was the first time I got to see the drunken extremes that Ashevillians can go to (with or without the aid of Sparks). I'd lived in New Orleans for five years at this point, and thought I'd seen drunkenness at its most extreme. I'd seen debaucherous drunks perform sex acts in the public square downtown. I'd seen a million frat-boy fist fights on the street. I'd once seen a drunk guy in a kilt stick fireworks in his ass and shoot them off at the cop car he was mooning. Never, though, until the Asheville Valentine's Day party, had I seen a group of wasted people acting so...*wasted*. Most of the crowd was in drag of some sort, including little ol' when-in-Rome me. Pizza was (supposedly) being served at the party, but the making of it quickly degraded into a vicious food fight, in the midst of which I got a hefty ball of dough to the face. And all the while everyone was slamming their citrus-flavored, enriched, malted energy drinks.

"It must be the altitude," I thought, watching in horror as a game of spin the bottle mutated into a pile of flailing, groping, glassy-eyed make-out monsters with orange tongues. Well, I thought, I guess there's only one thing to do, and cracked a Sparks myself. Twelve hours later I woke up in the bed of a complete stranger. I donned the torn up red dress I'd been wearing the night before and headed, wincing from the sunlight, back to Bigside.

Needless to say, the house was trashed. The food fight seemed to have left more dough on the walls than had ever made it into anyone's stomach. (Months later I ended up actually moving into the house and upon painting my room, the room formerly known as the "breakfast nook," I found flour coating the tops of all the windowsills.) In a raucous make-out session downstairs, Ted, a guy who lived in a broken van in the backyard, had ripped the bathroom sink from the wall mid-blackout, and immediately forgot he had done it. About fifteen minutes later, Ted discovered the dismantled sink and burst out of the bathroom yelling at a group of innocent bystanders, "That is so fucked up! Don't people know that this is our fucking *house*!?"

Spilled beer and garbage littered the hardwood floors of the antebellum house, as did the bodies of unconscious punk rockers in various states of undress and drag. Something obviously had to be done, so when the random traveling kids who'd slept on the porch offered me money to go to the store and buy booze, I ran down to the Exxon, still in my tattered Valentine's dress, and bought a bunch of Sparks. We distributed them back at Bigside and promptly cleaned the house and fixed the sink. The idea of drinking Sparks so that we could repair the damage done while drinking Sparks seemed poetic at the time.

Later on, after moving to Asheville and living there for a while, I started to get used to the massive Sparks consumption, used to jittery drunks with orange tongues. My friend Sonya came over the other day. "Whoah, hey Sonya," I said. "To what do we owe this pleasure?"

"I'm on a two-beer tour," she explained. "I'm going to all of our friends' houses and drinking two beers at each one."

"What?" I said. "You're going to be wasted!"

"Well," she said, "that's why at the last house I drank Sparks."

"What do you mean?"

"It evens out," she explained, meaning, of course, that Sparks' alcohol is counter-balanced by its caffeine. I'd heard this logic before, but have since experimented with the orange devil enough to confirm that it's total bullshit. If it were true then you'd come out feeling as though you hadn't drunk anything at all. Instead, with the teeth-gritting, stomach-churning and anxiety that Sparks brings, I'd say that drinking it is more like fending off an attacker while you punch yourself in the face. Apparently though, many people, especially those in the ranks of the Asheville punk scene, kind of like feeling that way.

It wasn't hard for Sparks to sink its sucrose-coated claws into our town, either. All it took was for a promotional Sparks Hummer to drive around, distributing the stuff. According to eye-witnesses, the punks were lined up on their bikes trailing the sickeningly-colored tank down Merrimon Avenue, hitting up its crew for more cans of the stuff at each stop. After that the punks were hooked. Every time there was a daytime event that demanded both alertness and inebriation, like a picnic, or a May Day celebration in the park, or a self-declared two-beer-tour, or even a long walk, Sparks was there, distributed from someone's black courier bag. At the First Annual Asheville Punk Rock Scavenger Hunt, convenience stores across the North side were sold out of the stuff, leading some hard-up alcoholic alchemists to conduct experiments in my kitchen, formulating their own Sparks out of Night Train and Red Bull. Another time a touring hardcore band, in a caffeine/alcohol induced fit, got caught shoplifting some of the vile stuff at Food Lion. They were followed back to the Trailer, the lowest of all punk houses, where the cops proceeded to beat the shit out of two members of the band, then arrested them.

When drugs like heroin make their way into a scene, it's usually in isolated cases to be dealt with by the users' close friends. Sparks, however, is now as ubiquitous as Cherry Coke or Pringles, and the effects on the punk scene run deep. Already-ailing teeth crumble into little orange chunks, like Pop Rocks. Paranoia runs high, usually resulting in delusions involving other punk rockers trying to get at your supply of Sparks. Even the music is getting jumpier and more disjointed. It seems like The Establishment has really done it this time, sunk its over-sweetened claws into the underground in order to take out any dissidence not already quelled by crack or heroin. Local punk scribe Blair Menace, seeing the damage that Sparks was doing around him, wrote a threatening letter to the 211 Company, progenitors of Sparks, saying something along the lines of "You fucking assholes, how dare you do this to my friends?" To my knowledge, he has yet to get a response.

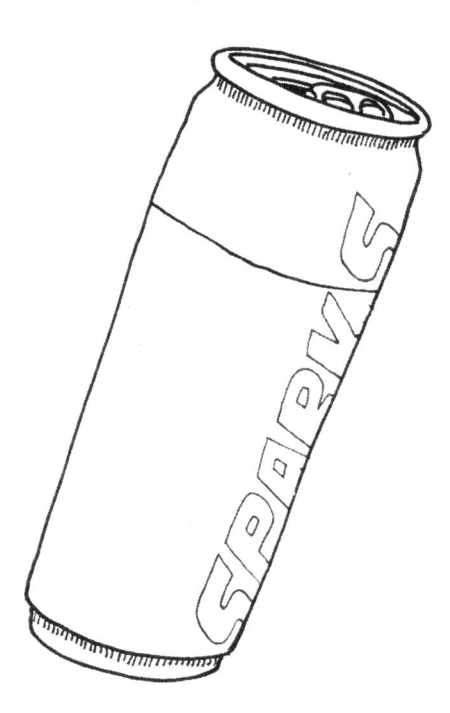

CRACK

I WAS OUTSIDE of the Yellow House, trying to loosen a 220 wire from the fuse box, when the tip of my screwdriver snapped off.

"Oh, goddamnit," I said, which drew the attention of a passing bum. The guy was walking through the yard about ten feet away and stopped to look at me from underneath his battered ball cap.

"Man, what're you doin' that for?" he asked.

I looked at him, then back at the fuse box, and down at my broken screwdriver and the pile of copper wiring at my feet. "I don't know what you're talking about," I mumbled.

"Aw, I see," he said. "You tryin' to get that copper."

"Yeah," I shrugged. "I am."

"Man, you don't want to be messin' with that. C'mon, I got some Sparks. We can go over by the creek and drink 'em."

"Naw, I'm straight," I told him.

"Suit yourself, then," he said and continued on his way to the disgusting creek that trickles out of drainage tunnels from beneath downtown. Going with the guy actually sounded like a lot more fun to me than pulling wire. But I'd left my co-conspirator, Ted, inside the house, and I couldn't imagine him being too happy if he learned I'd given up my duties in order to drink by a sickly creek with some random homeless dude.

Giving up on the fuse box, I took my broken screwdriver and handful of other tools back inside, where I joined Ted on the third floor. The Yellow House was huge, an old collective punk house where everyone had been evicted five years earlier by a hippie landlord with dollar signs in his eyes, hoping to cash in on the Asheville land boom. Other old houses had become boutiques, bead shops, make-your-own-pottery places, or whatever the trend-of-the-season was amongst the hippie-yuppie mountain culture that dominates Asheville. The Yellow House, however, sat empty, a great castle of yellow cement blocks that pale a little more with the passing of each summer. Inside, a lot of the art was left behind by the former tenants: anarcho-leaning Xerox collages and drunkenly-scrawled graffiti about overthrowing capitalism. Ted even found an antiquated can of Pabst stashed in the ceiling of the basement, no doubt hidden away at one of hundreds of punk shows put on in the place so that its owner could join the dancing.

Mostly though, the place was full of pigeons. Pigeon feathers and guano coated all of the rafters like the frosting on the worst cake ever. As I crawled through this muck, prying up the staples that held down the precious copper wiring, I began to seriously reconsider my decision not to go to college.

"You all right?" Ted asked.

"Besides the fact that I'm crawling through pigeon shit? Sure, I'm doing swell," I said. "But I don't think I'll be making a career of this, Ted."

We got through it, though. Working diligently, we pried up the staples, removed the outlets and junction boxes, all the while avoiding the windows and the prying eyes of the guys at the mechanic's shop next door. Their voices wafted up to us as we worked, reminding us that yes, the outside world still existed and yes, eventually, we would be allowed to re-join it. After a couple of hours we were sweaty, black with grime, and smelling like the birdhouse in a zoo. We were soldiers returning home, our copper bounty wrapped in big coils and draped over our shoulders like bandoliers.

A couple of days later we were sitting on the porch, struggling to strip the wire, trying to yank it from its plastic cover. Our friend Valerie came over to ask for some help with her van. She took one look at us and at the nest of discarded insulation at our feet. Valerie started laughing.

"Wow, you guys rule. I haven't seen anyone do this since watching crack heads in the bay area," she told us.

"Yeah man," I said. "We're gonna score ALL the crack!" And we laughed.

* * *

I was sitting in my room, at my desk, when Ana burst in. Ana pays us fifty bucks a month to sleep in her broken van in our driveway.

"Ella says that I'm not a punk!" she yelled.

I gave her my best cock-eyed look of confusion. "Pardon?"

Ana explained that while I'd been out of town recently, there was a party at our house that involved drinking for twenty-four hours straight in celebration of some obscure Jewish holiday. None of the party's atheistic participants had ever heard of the holiday before, but they decided it was worth celebrating. (This seemed strange to me not because none of them are Jewish, but because having known these people for some time, I'd never known them to need an excuse for all-day binge drinking before.) Ana told me that at the height of the festivities, Ella had befriended some random guy at the party, and that they'd sealed their new bond with a friendly trade: He gave her crack, and she hospitably offered up the living room to smoke it in. *Our* living room. Ana yelled at Ella, which led to heated political debates amongst the drunken anarchists on the porch as to whether or not it was okay for Ella to have invited people into our house to smoke crack with them. According to Ella, Ana's outburst meant that Ana was no longer punk.

Wow, I thought. What grade are we in?

This isn't the first time I've been in the middle of these debates. It's as though the punks decided that smoking crack was okay as long as you're doing it ironically, as if it's okay to sit around smoking crack just because you're not some twitchy, yellow-eyed guy wearing mismatched Keds and trying to sell women's underwear from a garbage bag. I'm sorry to inform you, oh nihilistic suburbanite youth, but crack is not a symptom of that behavior; it's a cause. Yeah, I know, the drug laws and the war on drugs are completely insane, a thinly-veiled sham for punishing small-time criminals while the big shots continue to pad their pockets, but that doesn't mean that I'm going to go shooting dope under the I-40 overpass. Fuck Nancy Reagan and all, but if Nancy Reagan had a "don't put your head through plate-glass windows" campaign, I wouldn't go putting my head through plate-glass windows just for punk points.

* * *

Before moving to Asheville, when I lived in New Orleans, the crackhead was a constantly re-occurring character on the set of the urban drama. You couldn't buy groceries without seeing them screaming at each other in the middle of the street over some drug-based misunderstanding, or riding around on a bike that looks a hell of a lot like the one stolen from you a couple months back, only now with a crappy Rust-Oleum paint job, or trying to open the doors on parked cars, or snapping the cars' antennae off to use them as pipes. (This happened to my friend Shelley's truck again and again until the antenna was no taller than a Popsicle stick, probably incapable of picking up a radio station even if it had been broadcasting from the back of the truck itself.)

During Mardi Gras, mass arrests take place in New Orleans for things like urinating in public or drunkenness. These arrests, on Bourbon Street even, are one of the city's biggest revenue sources. Those who can't post bond have to await trial. One Mardi Gras, I too was arrested for some bogus charge. As I'd been crossing a street in the Quarter, a driver had not noticed the red light above him and screeched to a halt, about six inches from hitting me. I was already in a crummy mood and let out a knee-jerk, "Hey fuck you!" and gave his car a swift kick. Things like this happened to me almost daily, especially if I was working bicycle delivery. Tonight, though, was Mardi Gras, and all the rules were different. The streets were at critical mass-full of drunks, angry fratboys, scared tourists, punks, puppets, naked people, and cops, all waiting for something to happen. It was a bad time to be instigating fights, which I realized as soon as the guy jumped out of his car, ready to fight, screaming at me. Within a minute a couple of cops had me on the hood of their cruiser, not even caring what had happened. Soon I was in a holding cell without an ATM card, along with all the other unlucky guys who couldn't make bond. That night, most of these prisoners were a bunch of "usual suspects" types, many of whom were (surprise, surprise) crack-heads who'd been picked up by the local cops just to get them out of view of the tourists.

After several hours of everyone sitting around with their heads on their knees, getting used to their surroundings, my cellmates started talking. And guess what the main topic of conversation was? I'll give you a hint: It was *not* how anxious they were to repay their debt to society. They started with a kind of group forum about crack, about crack addiction, and about how when they got out of jail they were going to get their shit together, for real this time. Soon, though, the sober talk gave way to a funny story about a crack deal gone awry or something, which segued into another story about a clever cop-evasion, and soon there was a full-on pep rally about how great crack was. Or how great it was before they lost control, about how they'd been on top of the world, how they could do anything. Soon, two particularly quick-witted dudes were up in front of everyone else in the cell going through what seemed like a tag team comedy routine about crack, telling one hilarious story after another.

"Man, I could talk anyone into *any*thing."

"I could fuck like a million dollars, all night long…"

One of them got so wrapped up in his words that he seemed to forget what he was saying, his hand hovering in front of his face, fingers pointing up as though clutching a crystal ball on which the events of his past were being replayed. "And you know? If I wanted — a woman, if I wanted a job, if I wanted anything, the whole neighborhood bowed down and it was just pow-pow-pow, *anything and everything I motherfucking wanted*!" Soon, though, the past melted away, the illusion gone like so much smoke, leaving him back in the cold reality of the jumpsuits, bars and bricks around him. Everyone was still laughing at his antics, but he couldn't carry his enthralled audience through another romp down memory lane, and he cut it short, saying, "Thank you, you've been great. I'll be here all month." And he flopped down in the corner of the wide concrete cell.

People turn to crack out of desperation, because they've never had the feeling of being in control before, and because, even if it's fleeting, crack will give you that. And because crack is everywhere, a little devil floating on their shoulders, offering them the feeling (although fleeting) of being on top of the world. And it's not just places like New Orleans, New York or

L.A. Crack is reaching out well beyond the demographic of impoverished inner-city residents. When I was in Dublin, Ireland, visiting friends, I read an article in their newspaper about the rock having made its way onto the Emerald Isle. As my friend Declan was riding to work in Dublin at eight o'clock one morning, a car pulled over and the driver asked him if he knew where to go about scoring any crack. Until then, heroin had been the drug of choice for Ireland's down-and-out, hopeless set; according to the paper, one in every thousand Irish citizens were addicted to heroin. Where New Orleans had its amped-up crack-heads running around screaming gibberish, Dublin had doped-out zombies stumbling around in their socks, draped in grubby blankets and wandering out into traffic. I thought that perhaps crack would rise up in Dublin to fill the romanticized niche that heroin has filled in the U.S. amongst hipsters, artists and rockers. I pictured skinny, black-clad people with big hair and pointy shoes all smoking a rock behind the gallery while avant-garde musicians played jumpy, discordant, crack inspired jazz. But I wasn't holding my breath or anything.

* * *

Perhaps I don't even have the right to sit around and judge, though, since I too have given in to the allure of the crack rock and the charm of some of its twitchy, harried users. I tried it, once, when I was fifteen years old, at my first job ever. I was a line cook at the Fast Times Deli or, as the chronically-stoned fry cook called it, "the motherfucking *High* Times, man." We would sit in the back, behind the dumpsters and smoke copious amounts of pot, much more than my fifteen-year-old brain and body could handle, then I'd stumble back into the kitchen to try and hold it together enough to put the shrimp on the french bread. Once I got so stoned at work that I passed out right there, at my post by the heat lamp, and had to be dragged from the kitchen to the hallway by my co-workers, safely away from the eyes of the customers waiting for their shrimp po' boys and muffulettas. When I came to, I was facing my manager, Ms. Clara, a tough, squat black woman in her mid-forties. Clara raised her three kids by herself on her deli manager's salary. She ran the place fairly, but in a way that made it clear that her operation had no time for, say, a fifteen-year-old line cook who was too stoned to put the goddamned shrimp on the goddamned bread, or for that matter, even maintain consciousness. Clara was standing over me, not even waiting for me to open my eyes before tearing into me with a torrent of insults. So it went at the ol' High Times.

One night I was taking a grease trap out back to clean it when I heard a crackling sound coming from behind the dumpster. I went to investigate, hoping to find someone smoking "that stuff," as Johnny the prep cook called it. It was Johann, the Puerto Rican fry cook, giggling to himself behind the dumpster. He looked at me through glassy eyes.

"Hey man," he said, doing his best impersonation of an after-school special. "You want some of this?"

"Weed?"

"No, man, this isn't weed…it's *crack*."

I thought about it for a second. I was fifteen years old. My favorite author was Jim Carroll; my favorite movie, *Drugstore Cowboy*. "If I'm ever going to smoke crack," I thought, "doing it behind the grease dumpster at work when I'm fifteen is definitely the time to do it." I was a lot smarter when I was fifteen than I am now.

"Okay," I said. I don't even remember, really, what the physical effects were. Perhaps everything took on a crisp-seeming clarity. Perhaps it felt like anything I wanted I would get, just "Pow Pow Pow!" Maybe I came up with some really pretentious ideas for plays I was going to write or something.

I remember Johann telling me, "You don't want to get messed up with this stuff, man. You don't want to end up like me," which I found odd since he'd never smoked the stuff either; he'd bought it off of Daniel the fry cook, who I'd heard talking about it earlier, saying almost exactly what Johann had just said to me.

We went back into the kitchen. I felt high for about, maybe, twenty minutes. Then I felt kind of gross, and kind of like I wanted more crack. That was it. That was ten years ago.

* * *

Ted and I discussed the Ella issue while we sat on the porch, stripping our copper wire. We discussed crack in general, and how the guy who'd lived in my room before me had been asked to leave because he was smoking it all the time and never had any money. It's scary when the jokes aren't funny any more because they've struck too close to home. With every joke, there's someone, somewhere out there who's able to say, "That's not funny," and then tell you some tragic tale about how their brother died and that's why you shouldn't go making jokes about crack, or fung shui, or tree-sloth maulings, or whatever it was you'd been wise-assing about. This is how experience kills a sense of humor.

We struggled with the wiring, and by the time the crack conversation ended, our hands were cramped and sore from clutching our box cutters, and we gave up. The next night, Ted and I borrowed our roommate Robby's car. The car, a little Honda hatchback, was the only functioning car in a veritable junkyard of vehicles behind our house, and had been given to Robby by a family friend. We opened its hatch, which was covered in old bumper-stickers about caring for the environment, stuffed it full of the insulation-coated wiring, and set out to find somewhere we could burn off all of the plastic. We guided the little car down to the river district, where all of Asheville's sketchy mis-doings are acted out. We drove past the train yard where people hop out of town, past the bridge where folks have fires and drink, past the bridges where people have set up permanent camps, past the bridge where the lady lives in her car with a bunch of cats. We found an oil drum behind an abandoned warehouse, right by the tracks, and built a fire in the bottom of it with tree limbs and scraps of old palettes. Once the wood was going strong, we started dumping the wiring on top of it. It caught fast, shooting up purple flames and sparks that glowed unnaturally like a neon sign, filling the sky above the entire river district with a noxious, ominous black smoke. I felt like we were evil wizards, setting our black magic free on this sleepy mountain town.

"Wow," I said, looking up at the evil plume that we'd created. "We'll be able to sunbathe in this spot this winter."

It took hours to burn all of it. We drank a twelve-pack of Southpaw and tried to avoid breathing the fumes or thinking about the noxious poisons that we were releasing into the air. "I guess I'll just be a nihilist for this one day," said Ted. "Whew. Ok. I can do this." Trains rolled by as we poked our fire with sticks, and when the wiring appeared sufficiently seared, we hurled the charred strands out onto the concrete slab beside us. With the terrible deed finally done, we put the whole mess of copper and charred plastic into a bucket and tromped back to where we'd parked the car, covered with soot and reeking of burnt chemicals.

"I can't believe this is what my life has come down to," said Ted.

I looked at his greasy, blackened face, and at our pile of blackened wiring, sixty bucks-worth, tops. I thought about Ella, and Johann, and the feelings of hopelessness and nihilism that have led so many of my friends to conclude, "Oh, okay, I guess I'll smoke a bunch of crack now." And I thought about my other friends, the ones who get freaked out and aghast at the idea of crack, who always keep "The Crackhead" onhand in their stable of butts for cheap jokes. Maybe that's why we react so strongly, maybe it's because we know that with a few bad decisions, a few unlucky strokes, that that could be *us*, smoking rock and screaming at each other under the I-40 bridge, trying to sell people stolen Wal-Mart kids' bikes with crappy paint jobs, or telling stories in a holding cell in Orleans Parish Prison, remembering the good times when we had it all and were on top of the world.

MONEY

I WAS WORRYING about money today. I'd been working at a fancy bike shop in downtown Asheville adjusting the brakes and shocks on four thousand dollar mountain bikes and making barely enough to pay my rent. So, on my day off, I was just sitting in the coffee shop, having trouble reading because of money troubles.

It was a beautiful day, so I decided to bike around a little to clear my head. Unlocking my bike in the corner of the parking lot, I looked over a hedgerow at the group of tired-looking men and women that was chronically loitering on the stoop of the plasma center next door. I was worried about money, but not as much as these defeated faces who bum smokes off one another as they wait their turn to go into the sterile, fluorescent-lit waiting room, and answer weird questions about how many African men they've had sex with since 1970, and to have their bodily fluids taken out of them for a few bucks — enough for a twelve-pack, or half the water bill, maybe. Tops.

    I thought back to the single time in my life when I was part of that sad-eyed group huddled in the reception area, being patronized by a cast of perky attendants who maintain this thinly-veiled ruse that you are doing this as some sort of service for humanity, even though you each know the sad truth from both ends, which is that you'd do just about anything for twenty bucks right now and that the plasma is probably going to be used by the cosmetics industry, not to save any lives (according, at least, to unsubstantiated rumor). I remember being stuck and re-stuck by a bleached-haired phlebotomist, then sitting there, staring at one Drew Barrymore movie after another on the TV above me, while my low-pressured blood crept up through the little plastic tube. After they take your blood out, they perform whatever alchemy is used to remove the plasma, mix the red blood cells with saline, and then they pump it back into you. Since the saline is room temperature, about thirty degrees lower than what your body is used to, you leave the place feeling this awful, bone-shaking deathly cold, and there's nothing else to do but shuffle to the nearest coffee shop and spend about a twentieth of your blood money on a couple of cups of coffee to get your body warmth back up to par.

    As I rode away from the plasma center posse, I started thinking about all of the other degrading things I've put myself through for money, and how I hope I'll never go through most of them again. As a teenage runaway in Philadelphia, I leased out a few inches of my forearm to a testing company that scoured my skin then smeared baby lotion on it for a week. I once worked as the assistant of a carpenter who would go into each job site and not sleep until the task was finished. My job duties were made up partly of priming baseboards and filling nail-holes, but mostly of running to the store repeatedly to buy him pseudo-ephedrine (which, by mandate of

Pennsylvania law, you couldn't even get in its pure form, but only mixed in with a bunch of other stuff in the form of day-time cold medicine). Another time I was hired by a concert promoter to walk around the city stenciling the pointy-lettered logo of second-tier metal band "Megadeth" on the sidewalk with cans of pink aerosol chalk. After leaving Philly I drifted to the Midwest, where I was lucky enough to be employed at a toothbrush factory and a Subway sandwich shop that I eventually quit via phone from New York.

"I'm in New York," I said.

"Oh," said my co-worker. "Does that mean you won't be in at eleven?"

"Yes, that's exactly what that means," I said.

"Oh," she said. "Okay."

A pizza place.

A burrito shop.

A hot dog cart.

And the graveyard shift at an all-night coffee shop.

Later, re-creating my life once again in New Orleans, I worked as a stilt-walker at conventions where I'd be paid to dress up as a French clown, or as Uncle Sam, or a football player, and smile my way through a million inane jokes by convention-goers.

I performed a circus act/comedy routine on a stage outside of a Satanic Halloween Haunted House owned by redneck rock troupe "Pantera." I delivered sushi on my bicycle to strippers and uptight French Quarter art dealers. I sold fireworks to rednecks in rural Wisconsin. I worked on bikes and handed out flyers and for a while ran low-end return frauds, returning stolen merchandise to suburban chain stores for cash or credit.

Most of these jobs lasted under two months. I once held a job as a walking courier for less than eight hours. At that moment riding down the street in Asheville, North Carolina, away from the plasma center, worrying about money, I didn't feel the urge to ever do any of these jobs again. The only thing worse than looking for a job is finding one. Every job I've ever gotten has taken me by surprise, a quick flurry of forms, applications, and next thing I know some middle-aged woman is copying my ID and telling me her policy on theft. So many first days at jobs I remember, looking at my new funny uniform, and thinking: Now what the hell am I doing? I don't need to do this. If I didn't spend all my time here, surely I could figure out some way to get by without a dumb job. And then, inevitably, I would quit. I'd do my damnedest to get by without money: shoplifting, getting on food stamps, dumpster-diving pizza and groceries. And while I highly recommend all of these things — take advantage of the wastefulness of grocery stores, get food stamps, shoplift from corporations whenever possible — eventually I just want to buy something. I want to go buy coffee, or Otis Redding records. And then I start all over again.

I looked around me at the scenery as I came into downtown. At the car dealerships, at the new "Staples" store that blocked out the sky and was visible from all over town, at the yuppie health food superstore, at the faces of the frustrated cell-phone talkers in their SUVs trying to get over to avoid hitting me as I forced my bike up the hills of Merrimon Avenue. I looked at all of these people and thought that, despite the drudgery and toil of it all, all of my various money-making efforts have not affected their lives in the slightest. Nor have theirs affected mine. Capitalism is like some great hot-air balloon kept afloat by nothing but the fact that so many people believe in it. And if we suddenly stopped believing, it would tear a hole in the thing, and we would all fall back to Earth, shake our heads and say "*Whoah*, wait a minute, we're all just *people*. Maybe we should just all work things out and make sure everyone is fed and cared for. What the hell were we doing wasting our time in that hot air balloon way up in la-la land?"

But until that happens, we're all trapped in this system, struggling.

Thus, I was plotting what my next weird job would be. And after that I'd find another weird job and another and another, and maybe, god-forbid, some day I'll buckle down, go back to school, and look around to find myself with a career of some sort, which in the end wouldn't really amount to much of anything either. And so on and so on. We all pretend that this is a reasonable and natural order of things, and if we don't, if we try to drop out, because we don't really see the point in dressing up like a clown on sticks, or in spraying the word "Megadeth" all over the place, then we end up out on the street. Or perhaps we end up down there at the plasma center, bumming smokes off each other, watching our blood creep way up a little plastic tube. And leaving the place feeling a little bit colder than when we arrived.

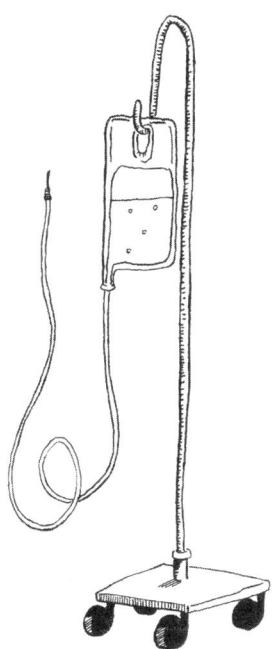

SUITCASES

HURRICANE KATRINA and her subsequent deluge left New Orleans a battered ghost town, "a surrealist landscape," my friend Alex said, adding that he doesn't think anyone's going to be selling any of "those prints with the melty clocks on them" anytime soon, since we could now look at the real thing for free. I had already moved from New Orleans to Asheville, but I was back there soon after the storm, helping friends tarp roofs and perform the ubiquitous Dance of the Dead Refrigerator, an exciting kind of waltz in which you hug your refrigerator, which has just spent all month unplugged and filled with food in the blazing New Orleans summer heat, and guide it, corner by corner, out to the curb, hopefully without letting the fridge open and vomit its rotten contents all over the sidewalk. Every day was like waking in a new place, a place where the power may or may not be on, where you may or may not still have neighbors, where there may or may not still be a fifteen foot fishing boat abandoned in the middle of your street, where uniformed men in Hummers may or may not stop you every block to ask you where you're going.

I went back to New Orleans with Cameron to see our friends, witness the desolation first hand, eat our share of Red Cross-provided Pop-Tarts and Fruit Roll-Ups, and take Cameron's stuff back up to our new home in North Carolina. Cameron's house in the upper Ninth Ward had faired well through the storm. The house next door was now leaning on his, and while Cameron was exiled to North Carolina, a friend had ripped his back door apart to retrieve some of his belongings for him. Other than that, though, the house was doing okay. This did not, however, prevent Cameron from being a totally grumpy bastard throughout our trip. That's just how he is.

I took the opportunity of being back in New Orleans (where I'd lived for six years before abandoning ship, fatefully, about six months before Katrina) to rekindle an old romance that had already proven doomed about a dozen times over. But now everything was different, right? New Orleans was a jumbled nightmare of wreckage, contractors, developers, hippies and exploding transformers. Maybe this crazed backdrop, combined with our own slightly unhinged mental states, would give our relationship what had been lacking before. Right? Well, yeah, probably not, but making out was fun again, and I didn't live there anyway, so why not? One day, after staying with the other member of said romance, I rode my bike, a clunky borrowed Schwinn, over to Cameron's place, where he'd been rooting through his heaps of broken recording equipment and trash-picked belongings, trying to figure out what to keep. He stood on the porch holding a broom, watching as I circumvented a heap of broken branches and locked the bike to the railing of his porch.

"I found a suitcase full of dead cats today," Cameron told me. I looked up at him, his face locked in an almost cartoonish frown, like Droopy Dog.

"Pardon?" I said.

"Cats. Dead ones. I was walking down the street and there was a suitcase on top of one of the millions of piles of garbage in the city right now. I thought, 'Man, that is a *nice suitcase*.' Then I opened it up and it was full of dead cats."

"Did you keep the suitcase?" I asked.

Cameron stared at me for a long time.

"No, man, I didn't keep the suitcase," he said, and went back to cleaning.

A few days later I walked into a work party for the Krewe of Eris. For the second year in a row, the Krewe of Eris would take to the streets, streets that looked much different than last year. Eris isn't like the other Mardi Gras Krewes; there are no beads, no flambeaux-guys, no creepy high-society secret balls, no floats even, just hundreds of ragtag freaks and anarchists who take over the streets for a night with drums and horns, with stilts and fire-breathing and costumes, and eggs. Lots of eggs. Colette, the curator of this chaos, had acquired hundreds of those brightly colored plastic Easter eggs. During that tumultuous period it was hard to find a grocery store in the city with vegetables or, for that matter, produce, but you could still get plastic colored eggs. Go New Orleans. The point of the work party was to write fortunes on little scraps of paper and put them in the eggs, which would be distributed during the Eris parade. Everyone at the party was slightly drunk or slightly high, sitting around picking their brains for words of wisdom to put on the scraps. I was promptly provided with paper and pen so that I could do the same. And damn, I just couldn't stop thinking about

Cameron, and that suitcase, and those cats, and how that guy just gets bad luck by the bucketful. A few days later his girlfriend would dump him and he'd leave New Orleans abruptly. A few months after that his bike would fall off of a boat on the Mississippi. The guy just invites misfortune and it's worked its way into his personality. There are some people in this world who you don't want to meet in darkened alleys; Cameron's the kind of guy you don't want to meet on a sunny spring day. He'd only bring you down. He just oozes this accursed luck. If you were to look at the deep lines on his forehead and how accustomed his eyebrows have become to sloping upward in defeat, you'd probably think: man, that guy looks like he just found a suitcase full of dead cats.

Sitting there, thinking about it, I watched Colette, our hostess, running around organizing baskets full of eggs. I remembered a story she had told me once about seeing a suitcase sitting in an alley one day in downtown Asheville. She didn't look in it and went about her business. The next day the suitcase was still there, but she still just let it be. The day after that the suitcase was gone, but there was an article in the paper about someone finding a suitcase full of ten thousand dollars in cash and a pound of cocaine. Remembering this, I picked up my pen and wrote on the little scrap of paper: "Always look in the suitcase. Sure, it's probably just full of dead cats, but maybe, just maybe, it'll be full of money and cocaine." When I put down my pen, someone else in the fortune-egg assembly line grabbed up the note, put it into one of the little pink pods, and threw it on the pile.

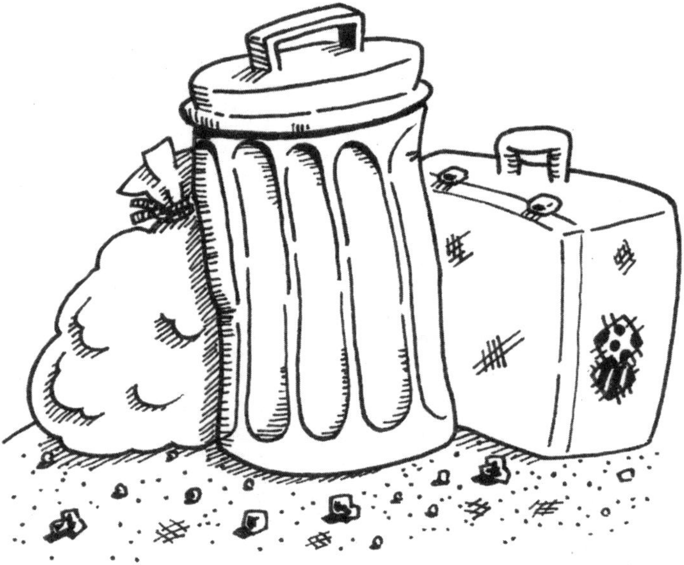

HILL PEOPLE

IT WAS STRANGE when I moved to Asheville from New Orleans. I'd never really expected to actually do it. Everywhere I've ever lived, people have warned me, "Be careful—this place is a vortex. You'll get stuck." Even in dull-as-dried-corn Iowa City people said this, and man, I didn't have a lot of remorse when it came to getting out of that place. In fact, I never believed it until New Orleans. Everywhere else I've lived there's come a day when *whammo*, I was just up and gone. In New Orleans, though, even the land formations are against you. It's overwhelming to stand in the city, thinking, I could leave, but to do that, I'd have to cross *all…that…water*. Nevertheless, I escaped. Soon I found myself in a new place, with new topography, new friends, doing things I never thought I'd do. In New Orleans, it isn't atypical to spend a night parading through the streets in an animal costume, or watching people burn all of their Christmas trees in the middle of the street. In Asheville, though, I was doing things I found truly strange, like going to college. Some days, waking up, it was hard to remember who I was. I'd have to remind myself, I'm Ethan. I'm not stilt-walker Ethan anymore, or bike mechanic Ethan, or hitch-hiking Ethan. I'm college Ethan now. In the mountains. Riding to school in the morning I would usually get there with that Talking Heads song "Once in a Lifetime" stuck in my head, then have to focus on filling out grant applications and such with David Byrne's cartoonish voice yelling, "Well, how did I get here?!" on repeat.

I never planned on going to college. If ever asked about it, I would spit clichés about the school of hard-knocks, or answer jadedly that the only reason I'd ever been on a campus was to steal things (and later to do readings). When I hit twenty-five, though, I'd moved from New Orleans to the relative calm of Asheville, North Carolina. Upon arriving I'd quickly gotten work at a bike shop, but later a broken collarbone left me unable to torque on wrenches (though the painkillers I was on made dealing with the agro mountain biking yuppies significantly easier). I was back in the same predicament I'd been in when I was seventeen in Iowa City — the "broke in a college town" predicament. My choices seemed to be either become a professional plasma-donor (a bad option for a pasty vegetarian with low blood pressure and a weak constitution), work at some restaurant for $5.75 an hour taking abuse from tourists, or go back to school. Eh, *voila*, one GED and a Pell Grant later, and I was stumbling around the campus of the local community college with the same frightened lost look that all the other freshmen had. My people.

As it is with most schools, the student body at A-B Tech consists of a pretty strange cross-section of humanity: There are the nursing students, proudly bopping around in their scrubs and orthopedic tennis shoes, stethoscopes swinging. There's a slew of working-class, redneck dudes — here because they have to take some safety training courses for work but are also required to take freshman algebra. And then there are the incoming freshmen, most of whom are seventeen or eighteen year olds that have just been tossed down the road from Asheville High so quickly that they don't seem to notice any change, except that here they can smoke.

My peers, I think to myself as I shuffle down the sidewalk alongside them, all of us clutching our new books and schedules.

As I walk up a hill to avoid the stairway crowded with chattering, cell-phone-clutching students, I think about how quickly we can reinvent ourselves, how the world can push us in one direction or another. One moment, it seems, I was ok with sleeping in the park and eating pizza out of the garbage all the time, next thing I know I'm applying to community college. It feels clichéd to outgrow my own rebellions and battles that I've clung to since childhood, but, after knowing the world is fucked up for so long it's become more and more obvious that dropping out isn't the way to make any change in it. And not only that, I've outgrown (or at least shied away from) other bits of the "fuck you" persona that I wrapped myself in for so long. Truth be told, these days I'd rather sit around listening to Otis Redding than Black Flag.

I started thinking more about the people that I am around on a daily basis, who live in my house or come over a lot. All of us have been pushed down the corridor called "Punk," a kind of amorphous umbrella term that refers to a certain attitude of rebelliousness and self-sufficiency, a musical taste, a style of clothing. It's what led us to end up together in life, for now at least, but that connection only goes so far. I wonder about all of the things they've been through that have knocked them in one direction or another, and about how much of it we've never talked about. I wonder how they would react if you were to strip all of that away, all of those identity markers and bits of culture that we pull together to make up the personalities that we show the world.

As I continue up the hill (which probably didn't take as long to walk up as reading this does), I think about what it would be like if we didn't have all of these common reference-points to work with, all of these "cultural compass-points" as someone once referred to them in a similar conversation. What if we couldn't all bond over conversations about Iggy Pop or 80s cartoon characters?[1] How would we react to things? How would we spend our time? What would the people closest to me do if they lived alone in the woods and didn't have to navigate choices of politics and music and wardrobe? What if all my friends had to deal with each day was climbing a big hill? How would they approach it? I started thinking about all of the new people I'd met in Asheville.

One of my current roommates is a guy named Robby. I think everyone has met at least one Robby in their life. He's the kind of guy who buys beer and records before he buys food. When his mom visited our new house, she looked into Robby's room and shouted, "My god! There's a sheet on the bed!" He's the kind of guy who, if you do your laundry with his, your clothes will come out dirtier than when they went in. And we all love him very much, but it's true. Robby's an easy

---

[1] Hey! If you don't relate at all to twenty-something punk culture, you don't have to feel alienated! Just scratch out the word "punk" and replace it with the subculture of your choice, say, "academic intellectual" or "pearl diver," and when I say things like, "Iggy Pop," replace it with "Foucault" or, "the bends." Nifty, no?

one: When confronted with the hill, he would just trudge up it. Every day. And he would complain about it, telling us how one of these days he was going to do something about it.

Then there's Ted. Ted is the doer, the mover, the kind of guy who doesn't care too much for books or movies, but will spend all day making the shelves in the house work a little better, so at least there's somewhere to put the books and movies. He's currently building a slip-straw house in the woods. He's not too good at holding a job, but he gets by pretty well without one, and you can often see him puttering around town in his veggie-oil van, babbling about solar-heated showers or something. Ted would spend a few days digging up the hill and installing a staircase, or, if he'd been drinking a lot of coffee that day, perhaps some sort of mechanical escalator fashioned out of Locust trees and vines.

And there's Nicole. "Dancin' Nicole," as a friend once called to her. Nicole, the whirlwind of energy, who is all smiles and excitement, bright patch-work clothes and tattoos of dancing vegetables. Nicole, who never runs out of fun ideas, who is in all the bands and talent shows and rock operas and musicals. Nicole, if confronted with the hill, would just run up it, then roll down it, then run up it again. Then she'd go pick berries.

But what about me? From day to day I feel torn between all of these personalities. I have my Ted days, for sure, where I'm moved to steal lumber, to build lofts and furniture, to weld fences and create everything I've ever wanted. But then I have days upon days of Robby days, when the tools sit, untouched, and I lie in bed and stare at the ceiling, and wait for inspiration that doesn't come. These days usually end with me stumbling home drunk. And then there's those oh-so-rare Nicole days, the days when I want to ride bikes to the top of mountains, paint murals, organize scavenger hunts and have dance parties.

I sit at the top of the hill, the real hill, the one at Asheville-Buncombe Community College, and think about it as the nursing students and freshmen and rednecks walk past me, talking about all of the compass-points in there lives, ignoring me. Eventually, it comes to me: on some days, sure, the Robby in me would bitch about the hill. Some days the Ted in me might get around to building the staircase, it's true. If the weather was good and things were going well, maybe I'd Nicole my way up the hill and roll down. But eventually I realize that while we all have our different moods, and we all might do something different from day to day. Most of the time, though, I would just sit on that hill, thinking about it too much for too damn long. Then I'd write a story about it.

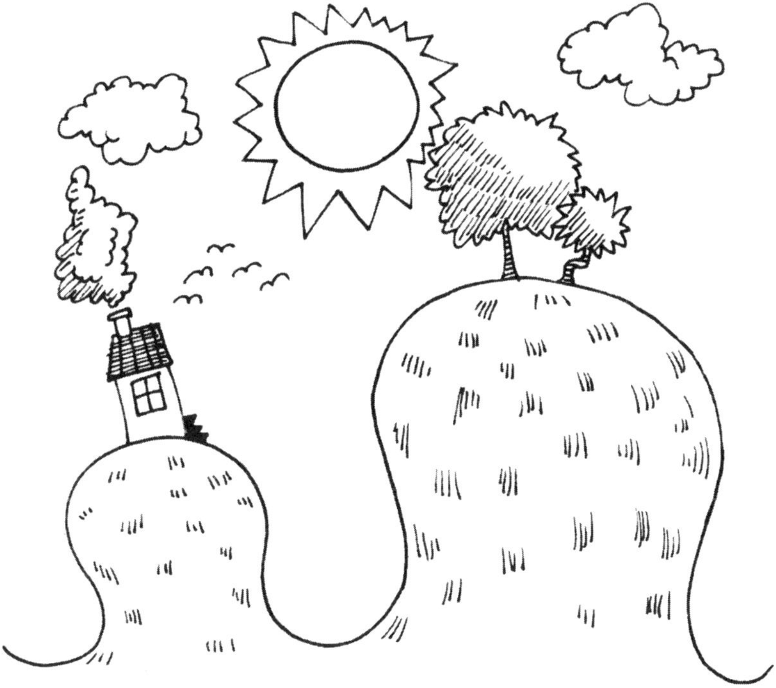

HIGH LIFE

The smoke stacks of the abandoned power plant rose above the Mississippi like some dark wizard's towers. I'd always seen the place from afar, but never known what it was. Then Colette and some friends threw a dance party on the roof, and I asked if I could play records. The party was underway when I arrived, and I made my way through the cavernous bowels of the power plant, up staircase after staircase, the path lit on either side by tea candles. Up, up, up, past huge machines like sleeping dinosaurs, until I came out on the roof, where thirty or so people were milling around, waiting *for music*. There were turntables set up already, and Christmas tree lights, powered by a generator which, through no small effort, had been dragged up the stairs by the party's organizers. This time I was just visiting New Orleans, back for the Fifth Annual New Orleans Book Fair. Looking at the turntables, laid out across an air conditioning unit, it made me remember how great this town could be. Soon my records were out of my bag and Irma Thomas's voice was wafting out across the river. The crowd grew, people drank and everyone started dancing. When the second DJ, Prince Pauper, began his set of old Jamaican forty-fives, things were in full swing. I went to the edge of the roof with Nicole, who had come down from North Carolina with me, and we sat on the edge talking.

"This is amazing," she said, looking out across the blown-out part of New Orleans known as Central City. Nicole had only been to the city a couple of times for a couple of days — once on tour with her old hardcore band, and once in college with her rugby team. This time was panning out to be a little more fun. For me, though, I was having trouble. I thought: What if she doesn't like my New Orleans' friends? What if she doesn't like New Orleans? When I voiced my concerns, she told me not to worry about it. We'd worked a booth at the book fair. All day we chit-chatted with people, and for Nichole, it was just chit-chat. For me, though, it was one long parade of old faces, of ex-girlfriends, ex-bosses, ex-roommates. It was almost too much to handle, almost enough to send me back into the car and back to Asheville. Questions like, "Is this a good book?" sounded, to me, like "What are *you* doing back here?" "I'm sorry I'm acting kind of weird," I'd said to Nicole. "It's cool," she said. "I'm just hanging out. You're the one from here. I'm not in the belly of the beast, but you know what the beast's been eating."

After a couple tallboys at the party, though, I was feeling better. "Things like this — this is why I love this city," I said, looking out toward the French Quarter. "Living here too long it can feel like it's killing you, but sometimes, it's the best place ever." We looked out across Central City and just sat there, listening to the scratchy records playing behind us.

Then the cops showed up.

At first it was a single cruiser in the alley below where we were perched. Prince Pauper cut off the music and lights and everyone stayed away from the edge of the roof, hoping they would just go away. Why would they care? After all, violent crime in the city had, over the summer, gotten so out of control that the National Guard had been brought in. Most of the cops in town were new to the job since so many had abandoned their positions during the hurricane, when called upon to do things that were *not* in their job descriptions. Why would these imported cops care about some little dance party on the roof of an abandoned building? How would they even know, in this city of celebrated madness, that that wasn't socially acceptable behavior?

Well…they did. Half an hour later, a handful of cops were up on the roof with guns and flashlights drawn, chasing partiers around like rats. I ended up on an edge of the roof behind a big vent that ran down into the depths of the building. Nicole was beside my friend Shanna, me, and two people I didn't know. We hunkered down and listened to the cops yelling at people, saying shit like "*Freeze before I pop a fucking cap in your ass!*"

Damn it, I thought, looking at the little hidden section we were all squatting in. Any second now some pissed off cop is going to come around the corner with a flashlight and threaten to pop a cap into our collective ass. Then Shanna made a discovery: The vent that we were behind, which was the size of a small room, was covered with a piece of sheet metal, to keep rain out. Between the sheet metal and the vent was a space just wide enough to squeeze into. I watched as Shanna wriggled up into the space, then the rest of us followed suit. We were pressed in there, against the grate of the vent, where we could clearly hear the cops in the building below, running around, rounding everyone up.

"GET THE FUCK DOWN HERE NOW!" we heard a policewoman shriek at a particularly drunk dude who'd crawled up on some perch in the building and passed out, apparently, with his shirt off.

"What?" he asked.

"I SAID GET YOUR FUCKING NAKED ASS DOWN HERE NOW!"

The wasted guy tried reasoning with her, making the mistake of calling her "sweetie."Ooh, I thought, bad move. I felt everyone else squeezed into the little space grimace, anticipating what was about to come.

"DO I LOOK LIKE YOUR FUCKING SWEETIE?!! IF YOU DON'T COME DOWN YOU'LL BE FUCKING FLYING DOWN. YOU HEAR ME?!"

This went on for a while, until the cops got everyone in the building into a line, making them walk down single-file. My friend Taylor, I'd learn later, was in the back of the line, hobbling along on crutches due to a recent foot injury. He'd been doing better, and tonight was the first time he'd been out of the house for a while. The cops, frustrated with his slowness, then threatened to pop a cap in *his* ass, and repeatedly called him "Crutchy," which they found very amusing. He walked down the seven flights of stairs, and messed his foot up even worse than it had been before.

The five of us squeezed in on top of the ventilation shaft just stayed as still and silent as possible. Man, I was thinking, we're going to hear these cops beat the shit out of someone! Later, other party-goers would give us flack for not just coming down, because hiding made us seem guilty of something more than dancing. The New Orleans cops, though, are not to be reasoned with, and I thought back on all the times I'd known them to arrest people for bullshit. I'd spent a night in Orleans Parish

Prison, sleeping on the floor with no blanket, charged with destruction of property after I'd kicked a car that had nearly hit me in a crosswalk. Friends of mine had been arrested for pissing outside, and forced to mop up the puddles of urine with their own coats. The keyboard player for a world-famous reggae band had his leg broken by the NOPD for "loitering" outside his own band's show.

Even after the cops were out of the building, none of us dared to move. It was silent, and we stayed there for a long time. Boy, I thought, here I am again, on the verge of getting arrested for trespassing. How do I keep getting myself into this situation?

I guess I got my taste for trespassing when I was seventeen and living in Philadelphia. I was enamored with the then-thriving Philly squatter scene. There were so many abandoned buildings there that the city couldn't even count them all. It was enough that if every homeless person in town had been given *their own building* then there would still have been thousands upon thousands left vacant. Loads of people were squatting, fixing up houses so that they had electricity, running water, nice gardens. I thought I'd get in on it and picked out a seemingly ripe house in West Philly. I went into the place, a huge two-story house in good structural shape, a few times, and patched up some holes in the floor and the busted backdoor. Then one day I went to put my own locks on the front door. I was almost done when the cops showed up. That probably would've been the end of it if I hadn't had the foresight to borrow a blue jumpsuit and tool-belt (complete with hardhat—since when do locksmiths wear hardhats?) from a friend. I'd been doubtful, but my friend had insisted on the disguise. "All you need is a jumpsuit and an air of confidence," he'd told me, "and you can get away with anything."

He was someone who, in his time, had gotten away with plenty (like walking out of a corporate hardware store holding a reciprocating saw, and building a house inside the supports of an abandoned train trestle, for example), so I took his word for it. The jumpsuit was made for someone about six inches taller than me and I didn't think that I made a very convincing locksmith. "Trust me," my friend had said, "You look great."[2] When the cop got there, I had zero faith that I looked great, but I decided to follow through with my bluff.

"What seems to be the problem?" I asked as I leaned over to talk to him through the passenger window of his cruiser.

"I got a call that someone was messing around at this place, but I guess it was you. You changing the locks?"

"Yup," I said. "Just changing the locks." I felt tiny in my jumpsuit, and I laid both arms on top of the car to keep my hands from shaking.

The cop called into headquarters to say that they'd sent him out over a locksmith.

"Alright," he told me, "have a good one."

"You too." I said. I didn't move.

"Thanks," he said. "I will if they don't send me out on anymore bullshit like this."

"Ha. Yeah," I said, still not moving. I was thinking about the jumpsuit and how on the back of it was a design of a skull with crossed wrenches underneath it. "This cop might buy a seventeen-year-old locksmith with a hardhat," I thought, "but no way is he going to believe that that's my company's logo." I had to move away from the car, though, so in possibly the most suspicious-feeling few seconds of my life, I slowly backed away

---

[2] Several years later I would see the truth in this statement again. I was living in Iowa City, Iowa when, according to the local paper, some guys in white jumpsuits stole a baby grand piano from a downtown hotel. They simply went in, jacked it up on a floor jack, and wheeled it out. Also the graffiti artist Banksy used the jumpsuit method to put his own art up in several big city art museums.

from the car and up the walk to where I'd been working, waving at the cop the whole time. He didn't think it odd, though, and left me to my business. I got the locks on, and even met the head of the neighborhood watch, who gave me his blessing in squatting the house, saying "as long as you don't smoke crack on the stoop, it'll be an improvement." I never actually stayed in the house, though, and when some friends did, they met the former illegal tenants of the place, who convinced my friends to leave by chasing them out with a three-foot pipe.

Another close call I had was in Columbia, Missouri. I was there hanging out with Taylor after our stint selling fireworks together. Two cops caught me sitting on a parking garage one night and wanted to haul me in because apparently I fit the description of "someone in the area who has been doing something." These were there exact words. *Someone who's been doing something.* I explained to them that I was a white guy of average height, average build with brown hair in a Midwestern college town. "Of course I look like someone in the area who's been doing something!" They didn't arrest me, and let me go, but somehow managed to find the phone number of my mother, whom they called daily. My mother was surprised to know that I was even in Missouri, and when I finally talked to her, she asked me to please get the Columbia, Missouri police to stop calling her.

This run-in on the parking garage led to the conception of "Parking Garage," a makeshift band that was going to play one show on top of every parking garage in Columbia. We flyered for the show, came up with a couple of sloppy songs, and were all ready to go, but the cops beat us there. When they arrived there was already a crowd of forty or so people standing around waiting for the bands to start.

"What are you all doing up here?" one of the cops asked.

"Uh," answered a kid named Dan, "we're watching the sunset."

The cops left and then stopped us from coming in with the equipment. Luckily there was a traveling circus troupe on the scene to entertain the crowd with improvised circus antics.

Another time in New Orleans, some friends and I hosted an art show in an abandoned building in the Ninth Ward. We spent days slipping into the building, a roofless warehouse on Royal Street, and putting up paintings, spray-paint stencils, murals, setting up food tables and a thousand tea candles to light the place. At dusk on the night of the show my roommate, Cassady, and I made a long, two-block walk from our house to the space with the biggest pair of bolt cutters imaginable, which Cassady had borrowed from the building supply place where we both worked. We'd tried wrapping the cutters up in a sheet, but that had made it look like we had a shotgun or something much more dubious than a pair of bolt cutters. So we'd walked to the space, struggling not to look at every car that passed, expecting the fuzz at any moment. We cut the lock off the door right at dusk, and had an art show. It went off without a hitch.

There's just something about reclaiming spaces, about going where you aren't supposed to be, about knowing that while the squares are watching TV at home, you are pulling back the curtains of reality, seeing what you aren't meant to, and turning every nook and cranny, every abandoned building, into your own playground. All it takes is imagination, maybe some beer, some tools, and nerve. Of course, things don't always go so well. As I was squeezed into that cramped space, I reflected upon my past trespasses. Less than six months had passed since my last run-in with the law. My friends Ted and Valerie and I were walking through Memphis, half-drunk and high after seeing Dead Moon play a show. We were passing the Memphis Zoo, on our way back to the house of a friend's friend. I was jumping around, excited, when we started talking about zoos. One thing led to another, and next thing I knew I was climbing up a tree and dropping in on the other side of the barbed wire fence, hoping to see the monkeys.

I didn't see the monkeys. What I did find was the house where the snow leopards were kept. "Hey," I hissed, "get over here." My friends were on the other side, in the shadows of a tree, looking up and down the street nervously.

"I don't know..." said Valerie, "I'm scared of heights."

"Ted," I said, "C'mon, man."

"I don't know..."

"C'mon man, they got *snow leopards* over here!"

"Really?"

"Yeah," I assured him, "they're right here."

"Okay, hold on," he said and climbed over the fence. Valerie headed home and we climbed to the roof of where the snow leopards were kept. Looking through a skylight, we saw one: a huge white beast surrounded, for reasons unknown to me, by lemon rinds. It saw us and stared, as enthralled as we were.

"It looks sad," I said. "I guess that's how I look when I'm in jail, too."

A few minutes later we climbed down the ladder again to find several of Memphis' finest, guns drawn, who took us promptly to jail for a night. Those are the breaks.

I thought my batting average was pretty good overall, and another arrest wouldn't tarnish it too much. But the Memphis debacle was so recent and the New Orleans jail is so terrible (at least it was before the hurricane, and I can't imagine that things have improved much since) that I wasn't quite ready to go back to it. After a good thirty minutes without any cop epithets, I ventured out of my hiding space and onto the roof, leaving the others in the tiny space. Creeping from shadow to shadow, I saw that some of the equipment was gone, including my bag of records, but most of it was still there. I ventured over to the edge of the roof above where the cop cars were. I could see that they were letting some people go, groups of two or three were making their ways out onto Tchoupitoulas Street.

Suddenly I heard someone go "Psst!" behind me. I turned to see the vague outline of a body climbing around on top of one of the dozen or so weird structures on the roof. He was just above head-height, and when he climbed down I saw that it wasn't anyone I knew.

"Hey," he said, "I'm a painter. I painted all this stuff up here." He motioned to the graffiti everywhere, which I hadn't noticed until then. "I know a back way out of here." "Ok…there's like six of us up here. First we need to get all the equipment and hide it," I told him. As quickly and quietly as we could, we moved the turntables, speakers and cords and stuffed them under a little tin roof that was covering some machinery. Next we went back to where Nicole, Shanna and the others were hiding. Whispering, I explained the situation. "So, come out *now*," I said at the piece of sheet metal, and suddenly four bodies appeared at the bottom of it, crawling out into the moonlight. In a single-file line, we made our way across the roof. We stopped at the makeshift bar that had been set up and all filled our pockets with the Miller High Life that had been left behind. Some of us opened one for the descent. If you're going to OPP, I recommend having as much beer in you as possible.

We made our way down, down, down through the guts and gears and innards of the great power plant. Candles had been set up on the rear stairwell, the one that we were on, as well, and as we passed them we bent down and pinched them out. We could hear the cops out front, still hassling people. There was some confusion finding a way out, but eventually we squeezed through a window and came out into the train yard behind the building. After that and a short tromp through a swampy field, we were in the clear. We headed to where we figured everyone would be after the cops were done with them: the nearest bar. Sure enough, there we found the organizers of the party, getting sloshed. It turned out that all of our hiding had been for naught; they'd let everyone go.

"Oh well," said Nicole, always the optimist, "it was still fun."

We hung out at the bar for a while, and then went back over to the space to retrieve the equipment. After hauling all of the turntables, speakers and the generator down the seven flights of stairs, we decided that it would be a shame to let all the beer go to waste, and went back up to the roof to take care of it. There were about eight of us now, and as we sat there, drinking the beer, looking out over the train yard, the river, and all of the tall buildings where thousands of corporate automotons waste away each day in their cubicles, I thought about all the times I'd gotten myself into these situations. I thought about the times I'd gone to jail, and about how we'd been run out of this building only an hour before by the cops but now were just sitting there, drinking beers and enjoying the scenery. I'm certainly not as brave as I used to be, not as willing to go hop trains around the country broke, or to go shoplifting everything I need, or to be content sleeping under a bridge. Now I'm in school, and I'm paying somewhat inflated rent to live in kind-of boring Asheville. Each morning when I wake up, I know where I'll lie down again that night, and sometimes I feel kind of like a quitter for that, like I should be out smashing police station windows, or being in sit-ins, or at least painting graffiti. I may have slowed down some, given in to some aspects of civilized society, but there will always be these moments of perfect, beautiful chaos in my life. There will always be the rooftop dance parties, the art shows in squats, the public freak-outs and unsanctioned parades.

I'll never give that up. The norms may have better teeth than us, but we have better senses of humor, and better dance moves. They may think that they're in charge because they have the tall buildings, but we can have tall buildings whenever we want. The cops might get us every now and then, but we still steal our high life at every chance we can. We'll all end up in the same place eventually. And I figure that that's all right, and I won't ever trade it for anything.

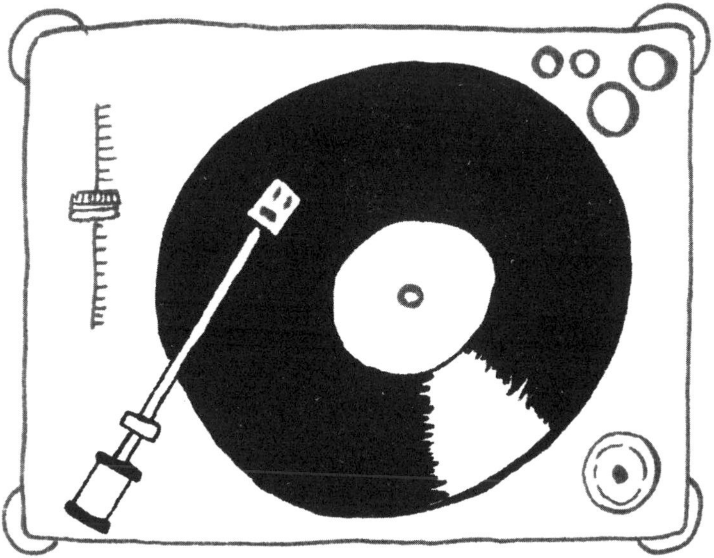

LEANING WITH INTENT TO FALL

TIMELINE:

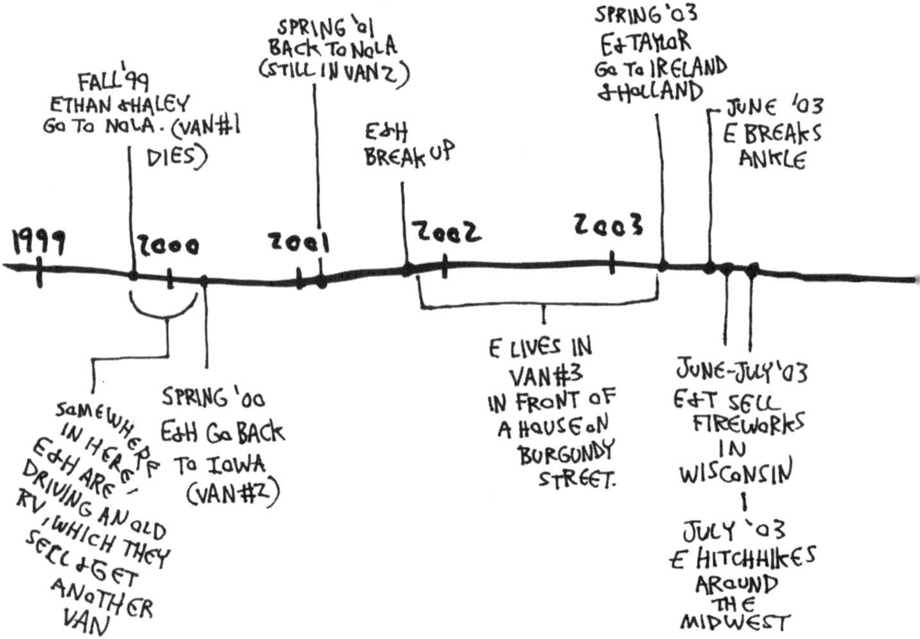

AUGUST '03, E & T HANG OUT IN MISSOURI & GO BACK TO NOLA

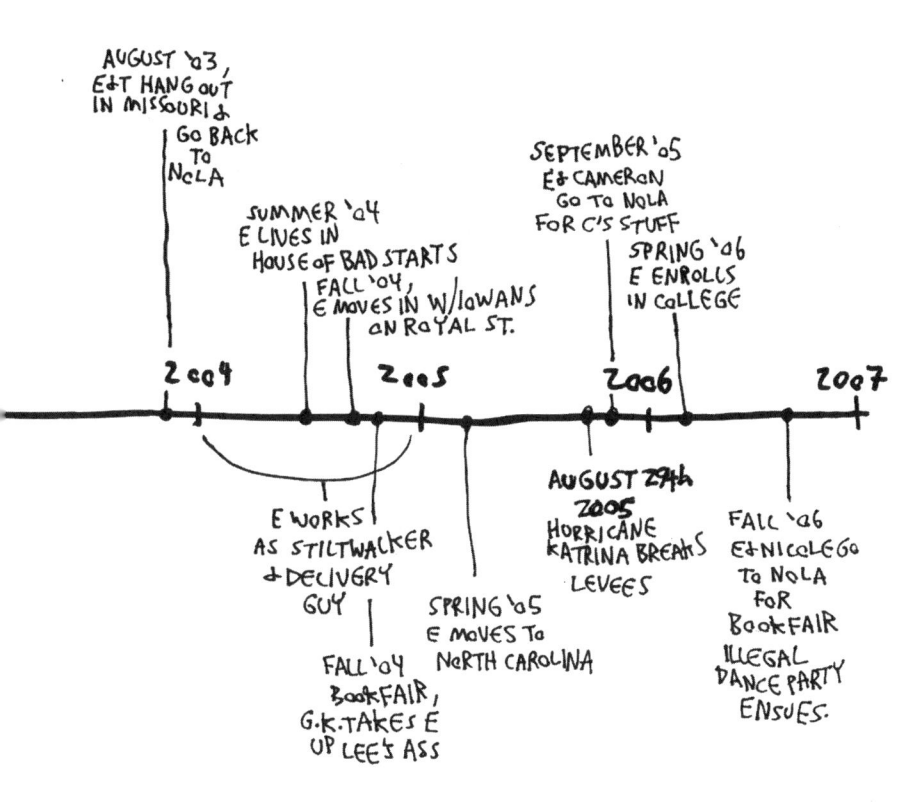

SUMMER '04 E LIVES IN HOUSE OF BAD STARTS

FALL '04, E MOVES IN W/ IOWANS ON ROYAL ST.

SEPTEMBER '05 E & CAMERON GO TO NOLA FOR C'S STUFF

SPRING '06 E ENROLLS IN COLLEGE

|---2004---|---2005---|---2006---|---2007---|

E WORKS AS STILTWALKER & DELIVERY GUY

FALL '04 BOOKFAIR, G.K. TAKES E UP LEE'S ASS

SPRING '05 E MOVES TO NORTH CAROLINA

AUGUST 29th 2005 HURRICANE KATRINA BREAKS LEVEES

FALL '06 E & NICOLE GO TO NOLA FOR BOOKFAIR ILLEGAL DANCE PARTY ENSUES.

ABOUT THE AUTHOR

Ethan Clark was born in Mississippi, two months before Reagan was elected president of the United States. During his childhood two films were made about the Klan within a mile of where he grew up. He got the hell out of there at age sixteen, pinball bounced around the country, and then lived in New Orleans for about six years. He now spends his time in Asheville, NC, working as a freelance writer, and living with a small, nervous Chihuahua with a difficult to pronounce Portuguese name.

He is the creator of the zines *Chihuahua + Pitbull* and *A Little Guide to Truing Bike Wheels*, and edited the book, *Stories Care Forgot: An Anthology of New Orleans Zines*.